THE PRESIDENTS

Editor

Fred L. Israel

VOLUME 1

George Washington 1789 – James Monroe 1825

Grolier Educational

SHERMAN TURNPIKE, DANBURY, CONNECTICUT

The publisher gratefully acknowledges permission from the sources to reproduce photos that appear on the cover.

Volume 1
J. Adams – New York Historical Society
J. Monroe – Library of Congress

Volume 2
J. K. Polk; A. Jackson; J. Tyler – Library of Congress
J. Q. Adams – National Archives

Volume 3
U. S. Grant – National Archives
A. Johnson; Z. Taylor – Library of Congress

Volume 4
B. Harrison; W. McKinley; J. A. Garfield – Library of Congress

Volume 5
H. Hoover; W. G. Harding – Library of Congress
T. Roosevelt – National Archives

Volume 6
D. D. Eisenhower – Library of Congress
L. B. Johnson – White House

Volume 7
B. Clinton – The White House
R. Reagan – Bush/Reagan Committee
G. Bush – Cynthia Johnson, The White House

Volume 8
T. Roosevelt – National Archives
B. Clinton – The White House

Published 1997 exclusively for the school and library market by Grolier Educational
Sherman Turnpike, Danbury, Connecticut
© 1997 by Charles E. Smith Books, Inc.

Set: ISBN 0-7172-7642-2
Volume 1: ISBN 0-7172-7643-0

Library of Congress number:
The presidents.

   p. cm.

   Contents: v. 1. 1789–1825 (Washington–Monroe) — v. 2. 1825–1849 (Adams–Polk)

   v. 3. 1849–1877 (Taylor–Grant) — v. 4. 1877–1901 (Hayes–McKinley) — v. 5.1901–1933 (T. Roosevelt–Hoover)

   v. 6. 1933–1969 (F. D. Roosevelt–L. B. Johnson) — v. 7. 1969–1997 (Nixon–Clinton)

   v. 8. Documents, suggested reading, charts, tables, appendixes

1. Presidents – United States – Juvenile literature.
[1. Presidents.]
E176.1.P9175   1997
973.099 — dc20

96-31491
CIP
AC

For information, address the publisher
Grolier Educational, Sherman Turnpike, Danbury, Connecticut 06816

Printed in the United States of America

Cover design by Smart Graphics

TABLE OF CONTENTS

VOLUME ONE

CONTRIBUTORS

EDITOR

Fred L. Israel received his Ph.D. from Columbia University. He has written several books for young adults including *Franklin D. Roosevelt, Henry Kissinger,* and *Know Your Government: The FBI.* Dr. Israel is also the editor of *History of American Presidential Elections, 1789–1968, The Chief Executive: Inaugural Addresses of the Presidents from George Washington to Lyndon Johnson,* and *The State of the Union Messages of the Presidents of the United States.* His most recent book is *Running for President, The Candidates and Their Images,* a two-volume work with Arthur M. Schlesinger, Jr. and David J. Frent.

Dr. Israel is Professor, Department of History, The City College of the City University of New York.

CONTRIBUTORS

Donald C. Bacon is a Washington-based journalist specializing in the presidency and Congress. He served as staff writer of *The Wall Street Journal* and assistant managing editor of *U.S. News and World Report.* A former Congressional Fellow, he is the author of *Rayburn: A Biography* and *Congress and You.* He is coeditor of *The Encyclopedia of the United States Congress.*

Hendrik Booraem V received his Ph.D. from The Johns Hopkins University. He taught social studies at Strom Thurmond High School, South Carolina, for many years. He has been Adjunct Professor at Rutgers University, Camden, Alvernia College, Lehigh University, and the State University of New York at Purchase. Dr. Booraem is the author of *The Formation of the Republican Party in New York: Politics and Conscience in the Antebellum North, The Road to Respectability: James A. Garfield and His World, 1844–1852,* and *The Provincial: Calvin Coolidge and His World, 1885–1895.*

Thomas Bracken received his B.A. and M.A., summa cum laude, from The City College of the City University of New York. He is currently enrolled in the doctoral program there, and he is Adjunct Professor of History.

David Burner received his Ph.D. from Columbia University. He is Professor of American History at the State University of New York at Stony Brook. Among Dr. Burner's many publications are *John F. Kennedy and a New Generation, The Torch is Passed: The Kennedy Brothers and American Liberalism* (with Thomas R. West) and *The Politics of Provincialism: The Democratic Party in Transition, 1918–1932.* He is also the coauthor of *Firsthand America: A History of the United States.*

Gary Cohn received his M.A. in Popular Culture Studies from Bowling Green State University in 1980 and has completed course work towards the doctorate in American History at the State University of New York at Stony Brook. As an Adjunct Professor he has taught history at The City College of the City University of New York and creative writing and composition at the C.W. Post campus of Long Island University.

Richard Nelson Current is University Distinguished Professor of History, Emeritus, at the University of North Carolina, Greensboro and former President of the Southern Historical Association. Among Dr. Current's many books are *Speaking of Abraham Lincoln: The Man and His Meaning for Our Times, Lincoln and the First Shot, The Lincoln Nobody Knows, Lincoln the President: Last Full Measure,* and with T. Harry Williams and Frank Freidel, *American History: A Survey.*

James B. Gardner received his Ph.D. from Vanderbilt University. He has been Deputy Executive Director of the American Historical Association since 1986 and Acting Executive Director of that organization since 1994. Dr. Gardner was with the American Association for State and Local History from 1979 to 1986, where he served in a variety of capacities, including Director of Education and Special Programs. Among his many publications is *A Historical Guide to the United States.*

Anne-Marie Grimaud received her B.A. from the Sorbonne, Paris and her M.A. from the State University of New York at Stony Brook, where she is currently enrolled in the doctoral program in American History.

Douglas Kinnard graduated from the United States Military Academy and served in Europe during World War II. He also served in Korea and Vietnam and retired as Brigadier General. He then received his Ph.D. from Princeton University. Dr. Kinnard is Professor Emeritus, University of Vermont and was Chief of Military History, U.S. Army. Among Dr. Kinnard's books are *Ike 1890–1990: A Pictorial History, President Eisenhower and Strategy Management: A Study in Defense Politics,* and *Maxwell Taylor and The American Experience in Vietnam.*

Robert A. Raber received his J.D. from the Law School, University of California, Berkeley. He retired from law practice and received his M.A. from The City College of the City University of New York, where he is enrolled in the doctoral program.

Donald A. Ritchie received his Ph.D. from the University of Maryland. Dr. Ritchie is on the Executive Committee of the American Historical Association, and he has been Associate Historian, United States Senate for 20 years. Among his many publications are *Press Gallery: Congress and the Washington Correspondents, The Young Oxford Companion to the Congress of the United States,* and *Oxford Profiles of American Journalists.*

Robert A. Rutland is Professor of History Emeritus, University of Virginia. He was editor in chief of *The Papers of James Madison* for many years, and he was coordinator of bicentennial programs at the Library of Congress from 1969 to 1971. Dr. Rutland is the author of many books including *Madison's Alternatives: The Jeffersonian Republicans and the Coming of War, 1805–1812, James Madison and the Search for Nationhood, James Madison: The Founding Father,* and *The Presidency of James Madison.* He is editor of *James Madison and the American Nation, 1751–1836: An Encyclopedia.*

Raymond W. Smock received his Ph.D. from the University of Maryland. He was involved with the Booker T. Washington Papers Project for many years and was coeditor from 1975 to 1983. He was Historian, Office of the Bicentennial, U.S. House of Representatives. In 1983, he was appointed as the first Director of the Office of the Historian of the U.S. House of Representatives. Among the major publications of that office are *The Biographical Directory of the United States Congress, 1774–1989, Black Americans in Congress, 1877–1989,* and *Women in Congress, 1917–1990.*

Darren D. Staloff received his Ph.D. from Columbia University, and he was a Post-Doctoral Fellow at the Institute of Early American History and Culture. He has taught at the College of Staten Island, Columbia University, and the College of William and Mary. Dr. Staloff is currently Assistant Professor of American History, The City College of the City University of New York. He is the author of *The Making of an American Thinking Class: Intellectuals and Intelligentsia in Puritan Massachusetts.*

John Stern received his M.A. from the State University of New York at Stony Brook, where he is enrolled in the doctoral program. His thesis is on Eugene McCarthy and the Presidential Campaign of 1968.

Edmund B. Sullivan received his Ed.D. from Fitchburg State College. He was Principal, New Hampton Community School, New Hampshire, and he taught at the North Adams and Newton public schools in Massachusetts. Dr. Sullivan was Professor at American International College and University of Hartford, and he was the founding Director and Curator of the Museum of American Political Life, West Hartford Connecticut. He is the author of *American Political Ribbons and Ribbon Badges, 1828–1988, American Political Badges and Medalets, 1789–1892,* and *Collecting Political Americana.*

Linda S. Vertrees received her B.A. in History from Western Illinois University and her M.A. in Library Science from the University of Chicago. She has written several annotated lists of suggested readings including the one for *The Holocaust, A Grolier Student Library.*

Thomas R. West received his Ph.D. from the Columbia University. He is Associate Professor, Department of History, Catholic University. He is coauthor, with David Burner, of *The Torch is Passed: The Kennedy Brothers and American Liberalism* and *Column Right: Conservative Journalists in the Service of Nationalism.*

INTRODUCTION

No branch of the federal government caused the authors of the Constitution as many problems as did the Executive. They feared a strong chief of state. After all, the American Revolution was, in part, a struggle against the King of England and the powerful royal governors. Surprisingly though, much power was granted to the president of the United States who is responsible only to the people. This was the boldest feature of the new Constitution. The president has varied duties. Above all, he must take care that the laws be faithfully executed. And also according to the Constitution, the president:

- is the commander in chief of the armed forces;
- has the power to make treaties with other nations (with the Senate's consent);
- appoints Supreme Court Justices and other members of the federal courts, ambassadors to other countries, department heads, and other high officials (all with the Senate's consent);
- signs into law or vetoes bills passed by Congress;
- calls special sessions of Congress in times of emergency.

In some countries, the power to lead is inherited. In others, men seize power through force. But in the United States, the people choose the nation's leader. The power of all the people to elect the president was not stated in the original Constitution. This came later. The United States is the first nation to have an elected president—and a president with a stated term of office. Every four years since the adoption of the Constitution in 1789, the nation has held a presidential election. Elections have been held even during major economic disruptions and wars. Indeed, these elections every four years are a vivid reminder of our democratic roots.

Who can vote for president of the United States? The original Constitution left voting qualifications to the states. At first, the states limited voting to white and very few black men who owned a certain amount of property. It was argued that only those with an economic or commercial interest in the nation should have a say in who could run the government. After the Civil War (1861–1865), the Fourteenth (1868) and Fifteenth (1870) Amendments to the Constitution guaranteed the vote to all men over the age of 21. The guarantee was only in theory. The Nineteenth Amendment (1920) extended the right to vote to women. The Nineteenth Amendment was a victory of the woman's suffrage movement which had worked for many years to achieve this goal. In 1964, the Twenty-fourth Amendment abolished poll taxes—a fee paid before a citizen was allowed to vote. This tax had kept many poor people, both black and white, from voting in several Southern states. And, the Twenty-sixth Amendment (1971) lowered the voting age to 18. (See Volume 8 for the complete text of the Constitution.)

In 1965, Congress passed the Voting Rights Act; it was renewed in 1985. This law, which carried out the requirements of the Fifteenth Amendment, made it illegal to interfere with anyone's right to vote. It forbade the use of literacy tests and, most important, the law mandated that federal voter registrars be sent into counties where less than 50 percent of the voting age population (black and white) was registered. This assumed that there must be serious barriers based on prejudice if so few had registered to vote. Those who had prevented African Americans from voting through fear and threat of violence now had to face the force of the federal government. Immediately, the number of African American voters in Southern states jumped dramatically from about 35 percent to 65 percent. In 1970, 1975, and 1982, Congress added amendments to the Voting Rights Act which helped other minorities such as Hispanics, Asians, Native Americans, and

Eskimos. For example, states must provide bilingual ballots in counties in which 5 percent or more of the population does not speak or read English. Today any citizen over the age of 18 has the right to vote in a presidential election. Many would argue that this is not only a right but also an obligation. However, all states deny the right to vote to anyone who is in prison.

Who can be president of the United States? There are formal constitutional requirements: one must be a "natural born citizen," at least 35 years old, and a resident of the United States for 14 years. The Constitution refers to the president as "he." It was probably beyond the thought process of the Founding Fathers that a woman, or a man who was not white, would ever be considered. The Twenty-second Amendment (1951), which deals with term limitations, uses "person" in referring to the president, recognizing that a woman could serve in that office.

How is the president elected? Most Americans assume that the president is elected by popular vote and the candidate with the highest number wins the election. This is not correct and may surprise those who thought they voted for Bill Clinton, Robert Dole, or Ross Perot in 1996. In fact, they voted for Clinton's or Dole's or Perot's electors who then elected the president. In the United States, the voters do not directly select the president. The Constitution provides a fairly complex—and some argue, an outdated—procedure for electing the president. Indeed, the electoral system devised by the Framers and modified by the Twelfth Amendment (1804) is unique. The records of the Constitutional Convention (1787) are silent in explaining the origins of the electoral system, usually referred to as the Electoral College. The several Federalist papers (Nos. 68–71) written by Alexander Hamilton in defense of the electoral system omit any source for the idea.

Under the electoral system of the United States, each state has the number of electoral voters equal to the size of its congressional delegation (House of Representatives plus Senate). Every 10 years, the census, as required by the Constitution, adjusts the number of representatives each state has in the House of Representatives because of population growth or loss. Every state always must have two senators. In the presidential election of 1996, for example, New York State had 33 electoral votes, because New York has 31 representatives and two senators. Alaska had three electoral votes, because Alaska has one representative and two senators. Since every congressional district must be approximately equal in population, we can say that the entire population of Alaska—the largest state in geographic size—is approximately equal in population to the 19th congressional district of New York City which covers the upper part of Manhattan Island.

There are 435 members of the House of Representatives. This number was fixed in 1910. There are 100 members of the Senate (50 states x 2 senators). This equals 535 electors. The Twenty-third Amendment (1961) gives the District of Columbia, the seat of our nation's capital, the electoral vote of the least populous state, three. So, the total electoral vote is 535 plus three or 538. To be elected president, a candidate must receive a majority, that is more than 50 percent, of the electoral votes: 270 electoral votes. If no candidate obtains a majority, the House of Representatives must choose the president from the top three candidates with each state delegation casting one vote. This happened in the 1824 presidential election. (See the article on John Quincy Adams.)

How does a political party choose its presidential nominee? Political parties play a crucial role—they select the candidates and provide the voters with a choice of alternatives.

In the early days of the Republic, the party's membership in Congress—the congressional caucus—chose presidential nominees. Sometimes state and local officials also put forward candidates. National party conventions where delegates were selected by state and local groups began by the 1830s. Each state had different delegate election procedures—some more democratic than others. Custom dictated that the convention sought the candidate. Potential nominees invariably seemed withdrawn and disinterested. They would rarely attend a nominating convention. Any attempt to pursue delegates was considered to be in bad taste. In fact, custom dictated that an official delegation went to the nominee's home to notify him of the party's decision and ask if he would accept. In the early years, convention officials sent a letter. By 1852, the candidate was informed in person. In the 1890s, these notification ceremonies dramatically increased in size. Madison Square Garden in New York City was the site for Grover Cleveland's 1892 notification.

By the first decade of the twentieth century, political reformers considered the convention system most undemocratic. They felt that it was a system dominated by patronage seeking party bosses who ignored the average voter. The primary system began as a way to increase participation in the nominating process. Candidates for the nation's highest office now actually sought the support of convention delegates. Theoretically, the primary allows all party members to choose their party's nominee. Most twentieth century conventions though, have seen a combination of delegates chosen by a political machine and elected in a primary. Today success in the primaries virtually assures the nomination. With few exceptions, the national conventions have become a rubber stamp for the candidate who did the best in the primaries.

The Campaign and Election. The presidential campaign is the great democratic exercise in politics. In recent elections, televised debates between the candidates have become a ritual, attracting record numbers of viewers. Public opinion polls continually monitor the nation's pulse. Commentators and writers analyze campaign strategies. Perhaps the winning strategy is to mobilize the party faithful and to persuade the independent voter that their candidate is the best. This is a costly process and since 1976, the general treasury provides major financial assistance to presidential campaigns. Public funding helps serious presidential candidates to present their qualifications without selling out to wealthy contributors and special interest groups.

Finally, on that first Tuesday after the first Monday in November, the voters make their choice. With the tragic exception of 1860, the American people have accepted the results. (See the article on Abraham Lincoln.) The election process works. Democracy has survived. Forty-one men have held the office of president of the United States. Each has been a powerful personality with varied leadership traits. Each had the opportunity to make major decisions both in foreign and domestic matters which affected the direction of the nation.

Join us as we proceed to study the men who helped to shape our history. We will also learn about their vice presidents, their cabinets, their families, and their homes and monuments.

Fred L. Israel
The City College of New York of the City University of New York

ACKNOWLEDGMENTS

Sir Isaac Newton, the seventeenth-century English scientist who created calculus, discovered that white light is composed of many colors, discovered the law of gravity, and developed the standard laws of motion, once said, "If I have seen farther, it is because I have stood on the shoulders of giants." He meant that he used the work of those who came before him as a starting point for the development of his own ideas. This concept is as true in reference books as it is in science.

The White House Historical Association (740 Jackson Place N.W., Washington, D.C. 20503) supplied all the full page color paintings of the presidents, except seven. They are used with the permission of the White House

Historical Association, and we are grateful to them for their cooperation. The painting of James Monroe is Courtesy of the James Monroe Museum and Memorial Library, Fredericksburg, Virginia; the William Henry Harrison portrait is Courtesy of Grouseland; the John Tyler painting is Courtesy of Sherwood Forest Plantation; the Benjamin Harrison painting is from the President Benjamin Harrison Home; Harry Truman's photograph is from the U.S. Navy, Courtesy Harry S. Truman Library; George Bush's photograph is Courtesy of the Bush Presidential Materials Project; Bill Clinton's photograph is Courtesy of The White House. All the busts of the vice presidents are Courtesy of the Architect of the Capitol.

Over three dozen illustrations are credited to the Collection of David J. and Janice L. Frent. The Frents are friends and neighbors. Fred Israel and I both want to thank them very much for allowing us to show some of the treasures of their unequaled collection of political memorabilia.

The authors of the biographical pieces on the presidents are listed in each volume. They have provided the core of this work, and I am very grateful to them for their cooperation. Dr. Donald A. Ritchie, Associate Historian, United States Senate, wrote all the biographies of the vice presidents. Few people know more about this subject than Dr. Ritchie, and we appreciate his assistance.

Maribeth A. Corona (Editor, Charles E. Smith Books, Inc.) and I have written the sections on Family, Cabinet, and Places. Dr. Israel's editing of our work corrected and improved it greatly although we take full responsibility for any errors that remain. In preparing the material on places, three books served as a starting point: *Presidential Libraries and Museums, An Illustrated Guide,* Pat Hyland (Congressional Quarterly Inc., 1995); *Historic Homes of the American Presidents,* second edition, Irvin Haas (Dover Publications, 1991); and *Cabins, Cottages & Mansions, Homes of the Presidents of the United States,* Nancy D. Myers Benbow and Christopher H. Benbow (Thomas Publications, 1993). We wrote to every place noted in this work and our copy is based on the wealth of information returned to us. It is the most comprehensive and up-to-date collection of information available on this subject.

There is no single book on the families of the presidents. We relied on the abundance of biographies and autobiographies of members of the first families. Also helpful was *Children in the White House,* Christine Sadler (G.P. Putnam's Sons, 1967); *The Presidents' Mothers,* Doris Faber (St. Martin's Press, 1978); and *The First Ladies,* Margaret Brown Klapthor (White House Historical Association, 1989).

The Complete Book of U.S. Presidents, William A. DeGregorio (Wings Books, 1993) is an outstanding one-volume reference work, and we referred to it often. I also had the great pleasure of referring often to three encyclopedias which I had published earlier: *Encyclopedia of the American Presidency,* Leonard W. Levy and Louis Fisher (Simon & Schuster, 1994); *Encyclopedia of the American Constitution,* Leonard W. Levy, Kenneth L. Karst, and Dennis Mahoney (Macmillan & Free Press, 1986); and *Encyclopedia of the United States Congress,* Donald C. Bacon, Roger Davidson, and Morton H. Keller (Simon & Schuster, 1995). I also referred often to *Running for President, The Candidates and Their Images,* Arthur M. Schlesinger, Jr. (Simon & Schuster, 1994). Publishing this two-volume set also gave me the pleasure of working with Professor Schlesinger and the Associate Editors, Fred L. Israel and David J. Frent.

Most of the copyediting was done by Jerilyn Famighetti who was, as usual, prompt, accurate, and pleasant. Our partner in this endeavor was M.E. Aslett Corporation, 95 Campus Plaza, Edison, New Jersey. Although everyone at Aslett lent a hand, special thanks go to Elizabeth Geary, who designed the books; Brian Hewitt and Bob Bovasso, who scanned the images; and Joanne Morbit, who composed the pages. They designed every page and prepared the film for printing. The index was prepared by Jacqueline Flamm.

Charles E. Smith
Freehold, New Jersey

George Washington

CHRONOLOGICAL EVENTS

22 February 1732	Born, Pope's Creek (now Wakefield), Westmoreland County, Virginia
6 November 1752	Received commission as major in Virginia militia
13 August 1755	Appointed colonel and commander in chief of Virginia militia
24 July 1758	Elected to Virginia House of Burgesses
5 December 1758	Resigned commission in Virginia militia
5 September –26 October 1774	Attended First Continental Congress
10 May–23 June 1775	Attended Second Continental Congress
15 June 1775	Chosen as commander in chief of the Continental army
2 August 1776	Declaration of Independence signed
27 August and 28 October 1776	Defeated at Battles of Long Island and White Plains, New York
26 December 1776	Victory at Battle of Trenton, New Jersey
3 January 1777	Victory at Battle of Princeton, New Jersey
11 September and 4 October 1777	Defeated at Battles of Brandywine Creek and Germantown, Pennsylvania
9 November 1777	"Conway Cabal" exposed; plan by General Thomas Conway to remove Washington as commander in chief of Continental army
19 December 1777	Established headquarters at Valley Forge, Pennsylvania
28 June 1778	Victory at Battle of Monmouth, New Jersey
19 October 1781	Accepted surrender of British General Charles Cornwallis, ending Revolutionary War
23 December 1783	Resigned commission as commander in chief
25 May 1787	Elected president of Constitutional Convention
17 September 1787	Signed Constitution
6 April 1789	Elected first president of the United States
30 April 1789	Inaugurated president
24 September 1789	Signed Judiciary Act
13 February 1792	Reelected president
4 March 1793	Inaugurated president
22 April 1793	Issued Neutrality Proclamation
7 August 1794	Issued Whiskey Rebellion Proclamation
19 November 1794	Jay's Treaty signed
27 October 1795	Treaty of San Lorenzo signed; known as Pinckney's Treaty
17 September 1796	Issued Farewell Address
1797	Retired to Mount Vernon, Virginia
14 December 1799	Died, Mount Vernon, Virginia

BIOGRAPHY

THE EARLY YEARS. The first president of the United States, George Washington, was born 22 February 1732 in Westmoreland County in Virginia's Northern Neck. The death of his father in 1743 left him an orphan. He was raised by his relatives and received a modest education from them. In 1749, he was appointed surveyor for Culpepper County in Virginia. Three years later, he inherited the plantation known as Mount Vernon from his recently deceased half-brother Lawrence. With the fees he earned as a surveyor, he was able to build his estate and ensure his financial security and comfort. On 6 January 1759, he wed the wealthy widow Martha Custis, to whom he remained happily married throughout the remainder of his life.

Washington's public career began in 1753, when he was 21 years old. Tensions had been growing between the colonies and the French and their Indian allies in the trans-Appalachian region known as the Ohio Territory. Washington was dispatched by Governor Robert Dinwiddie of Virginia to deliver an ultimatum to the French authorities, which involved him in a long and indirect trip through the region. The incidents of Washington's mission created some stir and were memorialized the following year in "The Journal of Major George Washington."

In 1754, Washington was commissioned a lieutenant colonel of the Virginia militia and was sent with 150 men to reinforce Fort Duquesne in the trans-Appalachian West. Realizing that the fort could not be held, he chose instead to build Fort Necessity as a line of defense at Great Meadows, Pennsylvania. On 27 May, he defeated a small party of French scouts. Although he was obliged to surrender Fort Necessity

on 3 July, he earned for himself further military fame at the very moment that the Seven Years War between the British and the French was beginning.

Washington's success at Fort Necessity earned him another military promotion in 1755. Barely 23 years old, Washington was selected by General Edward Braddock, the commander of the British forces in America, to serve as his aide de camp in his march against Fort Duquesne. The campaign proved to be a disaster. A mixed force of French and Indian soldiers ambushed the British forces and succeeded in killing many of their leading officers near the fork of the Monongahela and Allegheny rivers in western Pennsylvania. Despite the British defeat, Washington distinguished

George Washington was promoted to colonel of the Virginia militia in 1755. (Courtesy National Archives.)

▲ *George Washington took command of the Continental army at Cambridge, Massachusetts on 3 July 1775.*
(Courtesy National Archives.)

▲ *This famous painting by Emanuel Leutze shows George Washington crossing the Delaware River on Christmas Eve, 1776. His victory over the Hessians at Trenton was a great boost to morale.* (Courtesy National Archives.)

▲ *George Washington took the Continental army into winter quarters at Valley Forge, Pennsylvania in December 1777. They had very little food, blankets, or warm clothes, and they had to build huts for shelter. This is the famous painting "Prayer at Valley Forge."* (Courtesy National Archives.)

▲ *Baron Friedrich Wilhelm von Steuben, a Prussian officer of rare ability, arrived at Valley Forge and trained the army in drill, marching, and in bayonet practice.* (Courtesy National Archives.)

himself by his courage and his cool head under fire. His reputation as a military leader continued to grow. Upon Washington's return to Virginia, Governor Dinwiddie appointed him colonel and commander in chief of Virginia's military forces and entrusted him with the duty of defending the colony from French attack. Washington participated in the eventual conquest of Fort Duquesne in 1758.

COMMANDER IN CHIEF. Washington began his political career in the Virginia House of Burgesses in 1759. A champion of independence, he served in both the First and Second Continental Congresses. His most important service to the cause of independence, however, was his command of the Continental army during the Revolutionary War. Washington was chosen to lead the army on 15 June 1775 (not long after the skirmishes at Lexington and Concord, Massachusetts). He assumed command on 3 July. After losing to Washington's army at the Battle of Bunker Hill, the British evacuated their forces from Massachusetts and moved their operations to the middle colonies. For the next few years, the British regularly defeated Washington's untrained, ill-equipped, and understaffed army. Nonetheless, Washington was able to keep his army intact, avoid major defeats and engagements, and even score two morale-boosting victories at Trenton (26 December 1776) and Princeton (3 January 1777), New Jersey. After a brutal winter encampment at Valley Forge, Pennsylvania (1777–1778), Washington was slowly able to train and discipline the army of ragtag volunteers he had been given.

Washington's most important and impressive victory was at Yorktown, Virginia. With the help of French land and naval forces, he was able to surround the British army and force the surrender of its commander, General Charles Cornwallis, on 19 October 1781, bringing the Revolutionary War to an end. In 1783, he crushed a movement among his officers (many of whom had never been paid for their services during the war) to demand payment from the government at Philadelphia with the implied threat of a possible coup if they were not

given satisfaction. He gave a farewell address to his officers at Fraunces Tavern, New York, on 4 December 1783, and retired from public life to his Mount Vernon estate.

George Washington bid farewell to his officers at Fraunces Tavern in New York. He resigned his commission in 1783 and returned to his Mount Vernon estate. (Courtesy National Archives.)

General Charles Cornwallis formally surrendered to General George Washington at Yorktown, near the Chesapeake Bay in Virginia, on 19 October 1781. The British and German armies laid down their arms to the American and French soldiers, as the British band played an old English nursery song, "The World Turned Upside Down."

Although a final treaty of peace would not be signed for two years, all major fighting had ended. (Courtesy National Archives.)

THE PRESIDENCY. In the aftermath of Shays's Rebellion in western Massachusetts, Washington was urged by many of his new colleagues to leave retirement and support the growing movement to replace the ineffective government prescribed by the Articles of Confederation. Washington answered this call and presided over the Constitutional Convention, which met in Philadelphia in 1787. Washington threw his enormous prestige and reputation behind the newly proposed government as framed in the Constitution. Without his support and without the widely held belief that he would serve as the first president of the new government, it is doubtful that the Constitution would ever have been ratified by the states.

Inaugurated in Federal Hall in New York on 30 April 1789, Washington began his first term by presiding over the organization of the newly created federal government. During that summer, the first executive departments were organized. The Department of Foreign Affairs (later renamed the Department of State) was headed by Thomas Jefferson, the War Department was under the charge of Henry Knox, and Alexander Hamilton was named secretary of the treasury, the largest of the three departments. Early in his administration, Washington introduced the practice of cabinet meetings at which the heads of these departments met with him to discuss important matters of policy. With the passage of the Judiciary Act on 24 September 1789, which provided for a federal court system composed of a Supreme Court of 6 justices, 3 circuit courts, and 13 district courts, the creation of the government framed in the Constitution had been completed. The first 10 amendments to the Constitution, known as the Bill of Rights, were introduced and ratified in the fall and early winter of 1789.

HAMILTON'S ECONOMIC POLICIES. The most controversial, and the most important, issues of Washington's first term as president involved the financial and economic proposals of Treasury Secretary Alexander Hamilton. Hamilton, who had served under Washington during the Revolutionary War, sought to secure the financial credit of the federal government by appealing to the interests of wealthy investors and businessmen. He also proposed to use the federal government to promote manufacturing and industrial development. Both of these goals required a powerful central government, which Hamilton claimed the Constitution sanctioned under a "loose" construction of its terms. Hamilton's initiatives created strong opposition among southern and agrarian leaders, who rejected Hamilton's vision of an industrial nation with a strong central government. Under the leadership of Thomas Jefferson and James Madison, this "Republican" Party argued for a weak central government, bound by a "strict" interpretation of the Constitution, presiding over a nation of independent farmers. Although Washington strongly disapproved of party conflict, the growing dispute found him squarely in the "Federalist" camp led by Hamilton.

On 14 January 1790, Hamilton issued a Report on the Public Credit, dealing with the unpaid debt incurred during the Revolutionary War. The federal government had inherited from the previous government a debt of more than $40 million. Most of the securities representing that debt had been greatly devalued and had been purchased at a discount by speculators in the United States and Europe. Hamilton proposed funding these debts, and the interest due on them, at full value. He also urged that the federal government assume the burden of the unpaid war debts of the various states (roughly $25 million) under the same terms. By doing so, he hoped to cement the allegiance to the government of the wealthy commercial and investment interests in the nation that would benefit from this scheme, having bought up the outstanding debt at a discount. Jefferson and the Republican opposition objected to a plan that would reward speculators with taxpayer dollars. They also complained that Hamilton's scheme would punish those southern states that had discharged their war debts, and a congressional

FIRST INAUGURAL ADDRESS

Among the vicissitudes incident to life no event could have filled me with greater anxieties than that of which the notification was transmitted by your order, and received on the 14th day of the present month. On the one hand, I was summoned by my country, whose voice I can never hear but with veneration and love, from a retreat which I had chosen with the fondest predilection, and, in my flattering hopes, with an immutable decision, as the asylum of my declining years - a retreat which was rendered every day more necessary as well as more dear to me by the addition of habit to inclination, and of frequent interruptions in my health to the gradual waste committed on it by time. On the other hand, the magnitude and difficulty of the trust to which the voice of my country called me, being sufficient to awaken in the wisest and most experienced of her citizens a distrustful scrutiny into his qualifications, could not but overwhelm with despondence one who (inheriting inferior endowments from nature and unpracticed in the duties of civil administration) ought to be peculiarly conscious of his own deficiencies. In this conflict of emotions all I dare aver is that it has been my faithful study to collect my duty from a just appreciation of every circumstance by which it might be affected. . . .

By the article establishing the executive department it is made the duty of the President "to recommend to your consideration as he shall judge necessary and expedient." The circumstances under which I now meet you will acquit me from entering into that subject further than to refer to the great constitutional charter under which you are assembled, and which, in defining your powers, designates the objects to which your attention is to be given. It will be more consistent with those circumstances , and far more congenial with the feelings which actuate me, to substitute, in place of a recommendation of particular measures, the tribute that is due to the talents, the rectitude, and the patriotism which adorn the characters selected to devise and adopt them. In these honorable qualifications I behold the surest pledges that as on one side no local prejudices or attachments, no separate views nor party animosities, will misdirect the comprehensive and equal eye which ought to watch over this great assemblage of communities and interests, so, on another, that the foundation of our national policy will be laid in the pure and immutable principles of private morality, and the preeminence of free government be exemplified by all the attributes which can win the affections of its citizens and command the respect of the world. I dwell on this prospect with every satisfaction which an ardent love for my country can inspire, since there is no truth more thoroughly established than that there exists in the economy and course of nature an indissoluble union between virtue and happiness; between duty and advantage; between the genuine maxims of an honest and magnanimous policy and the solid rewards of public prosperity and felicity; since we ought to be no less persuaded that the propitious smiles of Heaven can never be expected on a nation that disregards the eternal rules of order and right which Heaven itself has ordained; and since the preservation of the sacred fire of liberty and the destiny of the republican model of government are justly considered, perhaps, as deeply, as finally, staked on the experiment intrusted to the hands of the American people. . . .

• *George Washington faced the tremendous task of launching a new nation which stretched from the Atlantic Ocean to the Missouri River and from the Great Lakes to Spanish-held Florida, a territory equal to all of western Europe including the British Isles. The United States had a population of just under 4 million which included 700,000 slaves. Ninety percent of the people were farmers. It is unlikely that the new government could have started if Washington had not agreed to serve as president. The first inaugural address was delivered in the Senate chamber housed in Federal Hall, New York City on 30 April 1789.*

President Washington appointed Alexander Hamilton as secretary of the treasury. He argued for a strong central government, and this put him at odds with Thomas Jefferson and James Madison. (Courtesy National Archives.)

PROCLAMATION ON THE WHISKEY REBELLION

Whereas combinations to defeat the execution of the laws laying duties upon spirits distilled within the United States and upon stills have from the time of the commencement of those laws existed in some of the western parts of Pennsylvania; and

Whereas the said combinations, proceeding in a manner subversive equally of the just authority of government and of the rights of individuals, have hitherto effected their dangerous and criminal purpose by the influence of certain irregular meetings whose proceedings have tended to encourage and uphold the spirit of opposition by misrepresentations of the laws calculated to render them odious; . . . by going to their houses in the night, gaining admittance by force, taking away their papers, and committing other outrages, employing for these unwarrantable purposes the agency of armed banditti disguised in such manner as for the most part to escape discovery; and

Whereas the endeavors of the Legislature to obviate objections to the said laws by lowering the duties and by other alterations conducive to the convenience of those whom they immediately affect (though they have given satisfaction in other quarters), and the endeavors of the executive officers to conciliate a compliance with the laws by explanations, by forbearance, and even by particular accommodations founded on the suggestion of local considerations, have been disappointed of their effect by the machinations of persons whose industry to excite resistance has increased with every appearance of a disposition among the people to relax in their opposition and to acquiesce in the laws, insomuch that many persons in the said western parts of Pennsylvania have at length been hardy enough to perpetrate acts which I am advised amount to treason, being overt acts of levying war against the United States . . . the motives of these outrageous proceedings an intention to prevent by force of arms the execution of the said laws . . . to withstand by open violence the lawful authority of the Government of the United States, and to compel thereby an alteration in the measures of the Legislature and a repeal of the laws aforesaid; and

Whereas by a law of the United States entitled "An act to provide for calling forth the militia to execute the laws of the Union, suppress insurrections, and repel invasions," it is enacted "that whenever the laws of the United States shall be opposed or the execution thereof obstructed in any State by combinations too powerful to be suppressed by the ordinary course of judicial proceedings . . . it shall be lawful for the President of the United States to call forth the militia of such State to suppress such combinations and to cause the laws to be duly executed. And if the militia of a State where such combinations may happen shall refuse or be insufficient to suppress the same, it shall not be lawful for the President, if the Legislature of the United States shall not be in session, to call forth and employ such numbers of the militia of any other State or States most convenient thereto as may be necessary; and the use of the militia so to be called forth may be continued, if necessary, until the expiration of thirty days after the commencement of the ensuing session: *Provided always,* That whenever it may be necessary in the judgment of the President to use the military force hereby directed to be called forth, the President shall forthwith, and previous thereto, by proclamation, command such insurgents to disperse and retire peaceably to their respective abodes within a limited time.". . .

• *The Whiskey Rebellion, an uprising by farmers in western Pennsylvania against a federal whiskey tax, challenged the authority of the new government. President Washington's response was swift and decisive. He sent an overwhelming force to bring peace to the region, disperse the rebels, and enforce the law. He accompanied the troops part of the way there.*

deadlock began. Finally, in the summer of 1790, a compromise was reached between Jefferson and Hamilton. Jefferson agreed to allow the funding and assumption of the war debt. In exchange, Hamilton promised that the future and permanent location of the federal government would be on the shores of Virginia's Potomac River.

In the winter of 1790–1791, Hamilton submitted a report calling for the creation of a national bank, to be modeled roughly on the Bank of England. The Bank of the United States would hold government deposits, serve as the financial agent of the Treasury, and issue bank notes that could serve as a medium of circulation. One quarter of the Bank's stock was to be held by the government, which would also appoint 5 of the 25 members of the Bank's board of directors. Moreover, bank stock could be purchased with government bonds at a discount, thus ensuring the participation of large commercial investors. In a written argument solicited by Washington, Jefferson objected that the measure assumed that the federal government had powers that were not in fact authorized under a strict interpretation of the Constitution. Nonetheless, Washington signed the measure into law.

In December 1791, Hamilton submitted a Report on Manufactures to Congress in which he called for protective tariffs, federally funded internal improvements to roads and waterways, and various financial rewards for technological innovation and industrial development. With such federal aid, Hamilton argued, businessmen would be able to combine the capital available in government securities and national bank stock and the untapped labor of unemployed women and children to create a manufacturing base to rival that of Great Britain, France, and other great powers. Although Hamilton's proposals were not acted on at this time, they would reemerge as important policies in the following century.

THE WHISKEY REBELLION. One of the results of the financial policies of Washington's administration was that the national debt skyrocketed to more than $80 million. At Hamilton's prompting,

on 3 March 1791, Congress enacted an excise tax on distilled liquor which, in addition to the existing tariffs, would help raise the necessary revenues to meet the government's financial obligations. This rather hefty tax (almost a quarter of the net price of a gallon of whiskey) proved immensely unpopular with the cash-poor farmers in the western regions of the South and in the mid-Atlantic states. Given the existing closure of the Mississippi River to U.S. shipping and the terrible state of the roads, distilling their surplus grain into whiskey was the only suitable way for western farmers to market their harvests. Resistance to this tax quickly grew in parts of the South and the West. In western Pennsylvania, the mails were intercepted, excise officers were intimidated, and the federal courts were disrupted by what came to be known as the Whiskey Rebellion. Pittsburgh was threatened with attack by the rebels, and a convention was held there in August 1792 that denounced the tax and promised to use every legal measure available to stop its collection.

Washington's response to the Whiskey Rebellion was swift and decisive. On 7 August, he issued a proclamation demanding that the rebels cease and desist in their activities. He called for a commission to offer amnesty to the rebels in exchange for their pledges of lawful obedience in the future. He insisted, however, that the excise on whiskey be enforced. When this proclamation proved unsuccessful in stopping the protesters, Washington called for an army of almost 13,000 soldiers from the states in the summer of 1794. The volunteers were placed under the command of General Henry Lee and were instructed to bring peace to the rebellious regions of western Pennsylvania. After a few weeks, Washington left the troops under the combined command of Lee and Alexander Hamilton. They marched unopposed through the affected areas, and with the capture of a handful of rebels, the crisis came to a close.

FOREIGN POLICY. Washington's greatest challenge as president came in the field of foreign policy. The French Revolution and the subsequent

European wars deeply divided U.S. public opinion. The Republican opposition embraced the French Revolution, whose struggle against aristocratic domination was thought to mirror the Jeffersonian struggle against Federalist elitism. Republicans argued that the United States should honor the mutual defense treaties it had made with the previous French Government and also aid the French in their fight with a hopelessly corrupt and monarchical Great Britain. In contrast, the Federalists reacted to the unfolding events of the revolution in France with shock and horror. They believed that the French Revolution represented the rise of terror, anarchy, and atheism rather than of virtuous republicanism. The Federalists saw Great Britain as the fortress of order and stability in an increasingly turbulent and chaotic European political scene. In addition, a far greater share of U.S. commerce was with Great Britain and its colonial possessions than with France. For all these reasons, most Federalists thought that the United States ought to side, in feeling at least, with the cause of Great Britain. Against both extremes, Washington steered a middle course of strict neutrality and impartiality.

THE GENET AFFAIR. The differences over foreign affairs became serious in 1793 when the newly proclaimed French Republic declared war on Great Britain. "Democratic Societies" arose throughout the United States in which largely Jeffersonian partisans celebrated the spread of the "republican" revolution overseas. These societies gave an extremely warm reception to Edmund Genet, the newly appointed French minister to the United States, upon his arrival in Charleston, South Carolina, in the spring of 1793. Genet had been instructed to negotiate a commercial treaty with the United States, but his actions had a far wider scope. He began commissioning U.S. ships as privateers to fly the French flag and capture British commercial vessels as "prizes of war." Genet commissioned a dozen ships, which often used U.S. ports as their base of operations. In all, these ships took roughly 80 British prizes, some of which

were captured in U.S. territorial waters. He also tried to organize military expeditions against British and Spanish possessions in Louisiana, Florida, and Canada. Throughout the spring and early summer of 1793, Genet remained in close contact with Jefferson and other Republican leaders and became convinced that the vast majority of Americans sided with the French in their struggle against Great Britain.

Not only was Genet threatening to draw the United States into a war with Great Britain, he was also violating the law of the nation. On 22 April, Washington had issued a proclamation stating that the United States was at peace with both France and Great Britain and ordered Americans not to act in an aggressive fashion toward either nation. On 5 June, Washington informed Genet that his military actions against the British violated the sovereignty of the United States. Although Genet promised to comply with Washington's proclamation, he continued in his course. In response, the Washington administration issued its Rules Governing Belligerents in August. The rules strictly forbade the equipping of French privateers and the organization of French military expeditions on U.S. soil. Genet refused to accept Washington's restrictions and demanded that he call a special session of Congress to judge between them in their dispute. If this special session was not called, he threatened to appeal directly to the American people themselves to settle the issue. Genet's outrageous actions alienated even Thomas Jefferson. In December, Washington presented all of his correspondence with Genet to Congress and demanded his recall as minister. The "Genet Affair" came to a close with the rise of the Jacobins in France, who called for his immediate return and described his actions as "criminal maneuvers." Fearing for his life, Genet sought and received political asylum from the very administration that he had recently attacked. He remained in the United States for the remainder of his life.

JAY'S TREATY. Relations with Great Britain were no smoother than those with France. Great Britain

John Jay was the first chief justice of the Supreme Court. President Washington sent him to Great Britain in March 1794 to negotiate a treaty. Jay's Treaty helped avoid a war with Great Britain. (Courtesy National Archives.)

had never honored its promise of 1783 to surrender its military posts in the American Northwest, and Indian wars on that frontier were widely attributed to British intrigue. In 1793, Great Britain issued an Order in Council that provided for the capture of shipping between neutral countries and France and its possessions. In the following months, the British successfully captured a large number of U.S. merchant ships on the seas, and by the spring of 1794 war with Great Britain seemed inevitable to many Americans. To avoid this war, in March 1794, Washington appointed Supreme Court Chief Justice John Jay minister to Great Britain. Jay was instructed to negotiate the surrender of the western posts, secure compensation for recent British privateers, and demand payment for slaves carried away by the British fleet in 1783. In addition, he was to seek a commercial or trade agreement with the British.

The treaty that Jay negotiated with the British authorities met only some of these requirements. The British promised to surrender their posts in the Northwest by June 1796 and to submit all boundary disputes to the arbitration of a joint commission. Arbitration by joint commission would also be used to settle the claims of U.S. merchants against British privateers, and to grant compensation to British creditors against their U.S. creditors. There was no provision regarding the removal of slaves in 1783 (Jay was an abolitionist), nor was there any protection against the British navy's impressment of U.S. sailors on the high seas. The commercial provisions of Jay's Treaty, as it came to be known, were not much more satisfactory. The United States was granted most favored nation status in its commerce with Great Britain and given the right to trade with India. The right to trade with the British West Indies was also granted, but only with small vessels and only under the condition that several of the most profitable staples (cotton, sugar, and molasses) not be exported to European markets. For his part, Jay promised to suppress all anti-British privateering from U.S. ports and dropped the long-standing claim that neutral nations such as the United States had the right to trade freely with belligerents in nonmilitary items. For their part, the British had still not revoked their Order in Council of 1793.

Although the provisions of Jay's Treaty were supposed to be kept secret until after the treaty's ratification by the U.S. Senate, in the spring of 1795 the Republican opposition "leaked" them to the press, and they quickly became widely publicized. The public outcry was enormous. The treaty was decried as a cowardly capitulation to Great Britain, and likenesses of John Jay were burned in public throughout the nation. With minor amendment, the Senate ratified the treaty in June 1795, but the Republicans continued to rally opposition to it throughout the rest of the year.

In the spring of 1796, congressional Republicans held their very first party caucus to decide what measures they would take to oppose the treaty. In March, they succeeded in issuing a demand from the U.S. House of Representatives that Washington deliver all of the pertinent papers and correspondence concerning the negotiation of Jay's Treaty. Washington refused to comply, claiming that only the President and the Senate had jurisdiction over foreign treaties. Although Washington established an important precedent by his refusal, he did not escape criticism. Representative James Madison hotly denied Washington's claim, and it appeared for a while that the House would refuse to appropriate the funds and enact the legislation necessary to implement the treaty. After much deliberation, and a famous oration by the sickly Federalist representative Fisher Ames, the House of Representatives on 30 April 1796 finally agreed, by a one-vote majority, to implement the provisions of the treaty. Jay's Treaty not only served to encourage trade with Great Britain and its colonial possessions, it also helped avoid a war with Great Britain that Washington knew the United States was not prepared to fight.

This original bust of George Washington was sculpted from life by Jean-Antoine Houdon, a French sculptor and painter, in 1785. It is on display at Mount Vernon. (Courtesy The Mount Vernon Ladies' Association.)

RELATIONS WITH SPAIN. Far less controversial than Jay's Treaty was a treaty that Charles Cotesworth Pinckney negotiated with Spain. Spain's control of Louisiana threatened to close the Mississippi River to the traffic of western farmers, who needed the use of the river to transport their goods to market. Signed on 27 October 1795, the Treaty of San Lorenzo secured for U.S. farmers the free use of the Mississippi River and the right to deposit their goods in New Orleans for three years. After that period, another site would be made available for the U.S. traffic if necessary. The treaty also confirmed western and southern boundaries of the United States as stipulated in the Treaty of 1783. For their part, the Spanish failed to draw the United States into a French and Spanish alliance against

Washington treasured this gift from Marquis de Lafayette. It is a key to the Bastille, the prison in Paris that was liberated during the French Revolution. It is on display at Mount Vernon. Lafayette was a French nobleman who offered his services to Washington during the American Revolution. He rose to the rank of major general. (Courtesy The Mount Vernon Ladies' Association.)

FAREWELL ADDRESS

. . . I have already intimated to you the danger of parties in the State, with particular reference to the founding of them on geographical discriminations. Let me now take a more comprehensive view, and warn you in the most solemn manner against the baneful effects of the spirit of party generally.

This spirit, unfortunately, is inseparable from our nature, having its root in the strongest passions of the human mind. It exists under different shapes in all governments, more or less stifled, controlled, or repressed; but in those of the popular form it is seen in its greatest rankness and is truly their worst enemy. . . .

There is an opinion that parties in free countries are useful checks upon the administration of the government, and serve to keep alive the spirit of liberty. This within certain limits is probably true; and in governments of a monarchical cast patriotism may look with indulgence, if not with favor, upon the spirit of party. But in those of the popular character, in governments purely elective, it is a spirit not to be encouraged. . . .

As a very important source of strength and security, cherish public credit. One method of preserving it is to use it as sparingly as possible, avoiding occasions of expense by cultivating peace, but remembering also that timely disbursements to prepare for danger frequently prevent much greater disbursements to repel it; avoiding likewise the accumulation of debt, not only by shunning occasions of expense, but by vigorous exertions in time of peace to discharge the debts which unavoidable wars have occasioned, not ungenerously throwing upon posterity the burden which we ourselves ought to bear. . . .

Observe good faith and justice toward all nations. Cultivate peace and harmony with all. . . .

In the execution of such a plan nothing is more essential than that permanent, inveterate antipathies against particular nations and passionate attachments for others should be excluded, and that in place of them just and amicable feelings toward all should be cultivated. . . .

So, likewise, a passionate attachment of one nation for another produces a variety of evils. Sympathy for the favorite nation, facilitating the illusion of an imaginary common interest in cases where no real common interest exists, and infusing into one the enmities of the other, betrays the former into a participation in the quarrels and wars of the latter without adequate inducement or justification. It leads also to concessions to the favorite nation of privileges denied to others, which is apt doubly to injure the nation making the concessions by unnecessarily parting with what ought to have been retained, and by exciting jealousy, ill will, and a disposition to retaliate in the parties from whom equal privileges are withheld; and it gives to ambitious, corrupted, or deluded citizens (who devote themselves to the favorite nation) facility to betray or sacrifice the interest of their own country without odium, sometimes even with popularity, gilding with the appearances of a virtuous sense of obligation, a commendable deference for public opinion, or a laudable zeal for public good the base or foolish compliances of ambition, corruption, or infatuation. . . .

• *This address was George Washington's farewell to the American people. His recommendations had a great influence on U.S. history. Washington explained that he had fulfilled his duty as president for two terms and would not serve a third term. This tradition lasted until 1940 when Franklin D. Roosevelt ran for a third term.*

Perhaps the best known part of the Address, which was published in newspapers and never orally delivered before the public, deals with his advice on foreign affairs. Although describing conditions of 1796, Washington's statements on isolation from European politics became the major course followed by U.S. foreign policy for more than one hundred years.

the British. Although Pinckney's success was largely due to the military weakness of the Spanish in North America (at one point he threatened to break off the negotiations unless the Spanish eased their demands), many observers concluded that he was simply a much better negotiator than John Jay.

On 17 September 1796, having declined to seek a third term as president, George Washington issued his famous Farewell Address. In it, he stated his reasons for declining to continue as president. He also reiterated the policies and principles that had informed his administration. He spoke out against the growing struggles between the Federalist and the Republican parties and warned of the growing factional and sectional divisions within the nation. He urged that his policies strengthening the credit of the United States of America be continued and sustained, for without sound credit the nation would never be strong enough to stand on its own. Finally, he warned the country to avoid permanent alliances with foreign nations. While temporary alliances might prove necessary and desirable, he said, the United States should steer clear of European political struggles and chart its own independent course in world affairs.

RETIREMENT. Having secured the establishment and the stability of the new federal government, Washington retired from political life to his beloved Mount Vernon. He continued to correspond with important public figures at home and abroad and was sought out at his estate by many dignitaries. When war with France seemed unavoidable in 1798, he was called out of retirement by President John Adams to assume command of the United States's military forces. The threat proved empty, however, and war was averted. Weakened by illness, George Washington died on his estate on 14 December 1799. His will provided for the freeing of his slaves, and the nation mourned the loss of the one man who had done more than any other to ensure its creation and survival.

VICE PRESIDENT

**John Adams
(1735–1826)**

CHRONOLOGICAL EVENTS

1735	Born, Braintree, Massachusetts, 30 October
1755	Graduated from Harvard College, Cambridge, Massachusetts
1770	Elected to Massachusetts General Court
1774	Elected to First Continental Congress
1775	Elected to Second Continental Congress
1781	Appointed U.S. minister to the Netherlands
1785	Appointed U.S. minister to Great Britain
1789	Elected vice president
1796	Elected president
1800	Ran unsuccessfully for reelection as president
1826	Died, Quincy, Massachusetts, 4 July

BIOGRAPHY

The nation's first vice president, John Adams played a critical role in winning the "minds and hearts" of the people during the American Revolution. As a young lawyer, the Harvard-educated Adams joined the Sons of Liberty and argued vigorously against the British Stamp Act of 1765.

A forceful speaker and debater, Adams became a recognized leader of the Continental Congress. He served on the committee that drafted the Declaration of Independence. During the Revolution, Adams represented the United States as minister to the Netherlands; after the war he became the first U.S. minister to Great Britain.

The Electoral College unanimously chose Washington as the nation's first president. To balance the influence of the Virginian, the second largest number of votes went to the New Englander Adams, who became vice president. Adams took his oath of office and delivered an inaugural address on 21 April 1789, nine days before Washington. While waiting for Washington to arrive in New York, the nation's first capital, Adams as president of the U. S. Senate expressed grave concerns over protocol and procedures. From his service in Great Britain, he preferred formal titles and ceremonies, which he believed would gain greater respect for the new government. Critics thought his suggestions sounded too much like the British monarchy Americans had just overthrown.

Adams considered the vice presidency insignificant and uncertain. "I am Vice President," he noted. "In this I am nothing, but I may be everything." More accustomed to participating in debates rather than presiding over them, he tried to discipline himself to remain silent. Yet often he became irritable and lectured the Senate about its procedures. Adams made the most of his authority to break ties in the Senate. His 29 tie-breaking votes were more than any other vice president cast.

Washington treated Adams cordially but rarely consulted him, and Adams loyally supported the President. When Washington was unanimously reelected to a second term, Adams had to overcome a strong challenge from New York Governor George Clinton to win a second term as vice president. By the time Washington chose not to run for a third term, political parties had emerged. Running as the Federalist candidate in 1796, Adams became the first vice president to achieve the presidency.

THE CABINET

SECRETARY OF STATE[1]
John Jay, 1784[2]
Thomas Jefferson, 1790
Edmund Randolph, 1794
Timothy Pickering, 1795

SECRETARY OF WAR[3]
Henry Knox, 1789
Timothy Pickering, 1795
James McHenry, 1796

SECRETARY OF THE TREASURY[4]
Alexander Hamilton, 1789
Oliver Wolcott, Jr., 1795

POSTMASTER GENERAL[5]
Samuel Osgood, 1789
Timothy Pickering, 1791
Joseph Habersham, 1795

ATTORNEY GENERAL[6]
Edmund Randolph, 1790
William Bradford, 1794
Charles Lee, 1795

1. Department of Foreign Affairs established 27 July 1789; renamed Department of State 15 September 1789.

2. John Jay was appointed by the Confederation Congress as secretary of foreign affairs in July 1784; held position until Thomas Jefferson became secretary of state in 1790.

3. War Department established 7 August 1789.

4. Treasury Department established 2 September 1789.

5. Office of Postmaster General established 22 September 1789. Post Office Department established 8 May 1795.

6. Office of Attorney General established 24 September 1789. Department of Justice established 22 June 1870.

(Courtesy National Archives.)

Alexander Hamilton (1755/1757–1804). Hamilton was appointed the first secretary of the treasury by President George Washington in 1789. During the Revolutionary War, he had served as Washington's secretary and personal aide.

In 1787, Hamilton, in conjunction with James Madison and John Jay, wrote *The Federalist,* a series of 85 essays which supported the ratification of the Constitution.

As secretary of the treasury, Hamilton advocated a strong centralized government. He argued that the federal government should pay all Revolutionary War debts, foreign and domestic, including state debts. He also recommended the centralized Bank of the United States, with a 20-year charter and assets of $10 million. Controversy over these proposals led to the party split between Federalists and Republicans. Hamilton's program was an immediate success in restoring the credit of the United States.

In January 1795, Hamilton resigned as secretary of the treasury but remained an advisor on major policy decisions. In the presidential election of 1800, he used his influence in the U.S. House of Representatives to break the deadlock in the Electoral College and have Thomas Jefferson elected over Aaron Burr. Hamilton regarded Jefferson as the lesser evil.

In 1804, when Burr was running for governor of New York, Hamilton said Burr was "a dangerous man, and one who ought not to be trusted with the reins of government." Burr challenged Hamilton to a duel at Weehawken, New Jersey on 11 July. Hamilton was fatally wounded and died the next day.

FAMILY

CHRONOLOGICAL EVENTS

21 June 1731	Martha Dandridge born	6 January 1759	Martha Dandridge Custis
1749	Martha Dandridge married Daniel		married George Washington
	Parke Custis	14 December 1799	George Washington died
1757	Daniel Parke Custis died	22 May 1802	Martha Washington died

(Courtesy Library of Congress.)

When Martha Dandridge Custis married George Washington, she was a wealthy widow with two young children: John (Jacky) Parke Custis and Martha (Little Patt or Patsy) Parke Custis. He treated them as if they were his own children and they called him father. As Jacky once wrote to him, "He best deserves the name of father who acts the part of one."

Patsy died before she was 17. Jacky was, at one time, Washington's aide during the Revolution. He also served in the Virginia Assembly. After his death, his four children remained with their mother, who remarried. However, George and Martha Washington were extremely close to the two youngest children: Eleanor (Nelly) and George Washington (Little Wash) Parke Custis. Nelly was 10 and Little Wash was 8 when their grandfather became president. They spent much of their lives with their grandparents.

Little Wash married Mary Lee Fitzhugh and their only child married Robert E. Lee. The Lees lived in the home he built at Arlington. That home is now the Custis-Lee Mansion, surrounded by Arlington National Cemetery.

The President's will left Mount Vernon to his nephew, Bushrod Washington, upon the death of his wife, Martha. Bushrod later became a justice of the Supreme Court. He also left large estates to Nelly and Little Wash. Martha Washington died two and one-half years after her husband and she left most of her possessions to Little Wash.

PLACES

After Washington's birthplace house was excavated in 1936, its foundations were covered with earth to preserve them. Its location and size are marked by an outline. The Memorial House, located near the birthplace site, is not a replica of the birthplace house, but rather a representation of a typical eighteenth-century, upper-class house. (Courtesy National Park Service; photographer: Richard Frear.)

GEORGE WASHINGTON BIRTHPLACE NATIONAL MONUMENT

RR#1 • P.O. Box 717 • Washington's Birthplace, Virginia 22443 • Tel: (804) 224-1732

Located on the Potomac River, approximately 38 miles east of Fredericksburg. Open daily from 9 A.M. to 5 P.M. Closed Christmas and New Year's Day. Admission fee. Handicapped accessible. Candlelight tours are available during a yearly Christmas open house. The site contains the Memorial House, the birthplace site, a Colonial herb and flower garden, a Colonial living farm, the burial ground, a visitor center, a gift shop, walking trails, and picnic areas. Administered by the National Park Service, U.S. Department of the Interior.

George Washington was born on 22 February 1732 in a U-shaped, brick plantation manor house located along the banks of Popes Creek in Westmoreland County, Virginia. He lived there for the first three-and-a-half years of his life, after which his family moved 80 miles up the Potomac River to Little Hunting Creek (later called Mount Vernon). The house burned in 1779 and was never rebuilt.

In 1858, the Commonwealth of Virginia acquired the plantation grounds and made plans to preserve and mark the site. Because of the Civil War, the plans were never carried out. Twenty-four years later, Virginia donated the land to the federal government, and in 1896 a granite memorial shaft was erected on the site. In 1923, the Wakefield National Memorial Association was established to recover and restore the birthplace grounds. Between 1930 and 1931, a Memorial House and a separate kitchen were built and furnished with eighteenth-century period pieces.

In 1932, on the 200th anniversary of Washington's birth, the site was officially opened to the public.

MOUNT VERNON

Mount Vernon, Virginia 22121 • Tel: (703) 780-2000

Located at the end of the George Washington Memorial Parkway (also known as the Mount Vernon Memorial Highway), approximately 16 miles from Washington, D.C. and 8 miles south of Old Town Alexandria, Virginia. Open every day of the year, including Christmas. April through August from 8 A.M. to 5 P.M.; March, September, and October from 9 A.M. to 5 P.M.; November through February from 9 A.M. to 4 P.M. Admission fee, with discounts available for senior citizens and student groups. After Hours Tours (private evening tours) are available for both small and large groups. For more information, call: (703) 780-2000, Ext. 301. A museum, two gift shops, a full-service snack bar, and a restaurant are located on the estate. Boat cruises to Mount Vernon down the Potomac River from Washington, D.C. are available from the Spirit of Washington *between mid-March and October; call: (202) 554-8000. A limited number of wheelchairs are available at the entrance, free of charge. Owned and maintained by the Mount Vernon Ladies' Association, a nonprofit organization founded in 1853 to restore and preserve the home of George Washington.*

Between 1754 and 1799, George Washington expanded the mansion at Mount Vernon and added the high-columned porch that extends the length of the east front, a distinct architectural innovation in its day. (Courtesy The Mount Vernon Ladies' Association.)

In 1674, George Washington's great-grandfather was given a grant of land for the Little Hunting Creek Plantation. Some years later Washington's father, Augustine, acquired the estate and settled his family there. After Augustine's death in 1743, Lawrence, George's half brother, married and then settled on the plantation. Lawrence later renamed it Mount Vernon after the English Admiral "Old Grog" Vernon,

under whom he had served. In 1754, two years after Lawrence's death, George leased the estate from his brother's widow. After her death in 1761, he became the official owner of the estate, and lived there until his death in 1799.

Mount Vernon grew from 2,126 acres to more than 8,000 in the 45 years of Washington's occupancy. He was his own architect, and he developed Mount

Vernon into one of the finest estates of its time. A total of 14 rooms are open to the public for viewing, including the bed-chamber containing the bed on which he died. The exhibition area contains more than a dozen outer buildings and over 30 acres of beautiful gardens and wooded grounds. The tomb where Washington is buried with his wife, Martha, and other family members is located across from a slave burial ground marked by a memorial to the slaves of Mount Vernon.

Mount Vernon, one of America's most popular historic homes, is the country's oldest ongoing national preservation project. Thousands of visitors pass through the gates each day to enjoy this unique historic site. Museum guides inside the mansion inform visitors about Washington's life and answer questions during the self-guided tours.

Washington learned of his election to the presidency in the large dining room at Mount Vernon. (Courtesy The Mount Vernon Ladies' Association.)

WASHINGTON MONUMENT

The National Mall at Fifteenth St., NW • Washington, D.C. • Tel: (202) 426-6841

Open daily, September through March, from 9 A.M. to 5 P.M.; April through August, from 8 A.M. to midnight. Closed Christmas. No admission fee. Free tickets are distributed daily to visitors on a first-come basis. They can be reserved in advance from Ticketmaster, call: (800) 368-6511. Handicapped accessible. Scheduled tours. For more information, write: Superintendent, National Capital Parks-Central, 900 Ohio Drive SW, Washington, D.C. 20242. A unit of the National Park System.

George Washington chose the site for the Washington Monument in 1783. It was to have been the site of a monument to the American Revolution. To the north, less than a mile away, is the White House; to the south are the Jefferson Memorial and the Potomac River. The Capitol is east, in a direct line, and the Lincoln Memorial is to the west. The monument towers over everything in the Capital; it is surrounded by more than 40 acres of beautiful, sloping ground.

On 19 December 1799, the day after George Washington was buried at Mount Vernon, a committee of both Houses of Congress was appointed to decide how to honor his memory. On Christmas Eve of that same year, Congress passed a resolution to erect a marble monument and proposing "that the family of George Washington be requested to permit his body to be deposited under it...." President John Adams did request this of Mrs. Washington, and she agreed although she admitted that she was sacrificing her individual feeling to a sense of public duty.

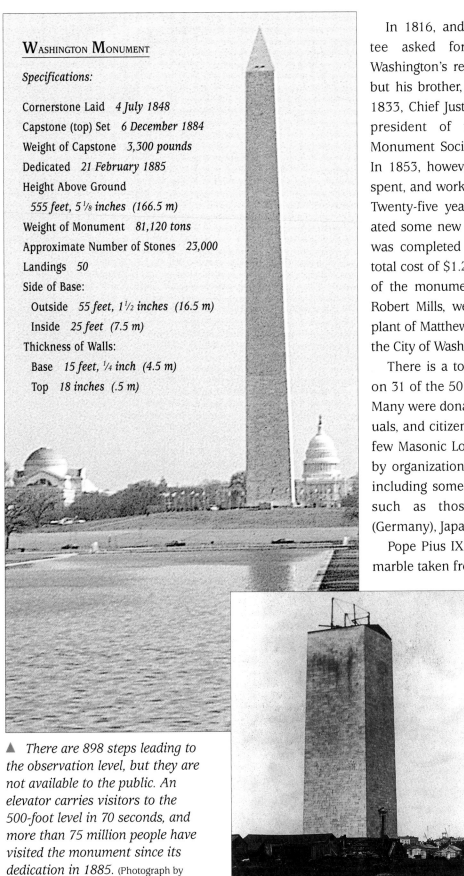

WASHINGTON MONUMENT

Specifications:

Cornerstone Laid   *4 July 1848*

Capstone (top) Set   *6 December 1884*

Weight of Capstone   *3,300 pounds*

Dedicated   *21 February 1885*

Height Above Ground
  555 feet, 5 $\frac{1}{8}$ inches (166.5 m)

Weight of Monument   *81,120 tons*

Approximate Number of Stones   *23,000*

Landings   *50*

Side of Base:
  Outside   *55 feet, 1 $\frac{1}{2}$ inches (16.5 m)*
  Inside   *25 feet (7.5 m)*

Thickness of Walls:
  Base   *15 feet, $\frac{1}{4}$ inch (4.5 m)*
  Top   *18 inches (.5 m)*

▲ *There are 898 steps leading to the observation level, but they are not available to the public. An elevator carries visitors to the 500-foot level in 70 seconds, and more than 75 million people have visited the monument since its dedication in 1885.* (Photograph by A. A. M. van der Heyden.)

In 1816, and again in 1832, a committee asked for permission to remove Washington's remains from Mount Vernon, but his brother, John Augustine, refused. In 1833, Chief Justice John Marshall served as president of the Washington National Monument Society, which raised $300,000. In 1853, however, all the money had been spent, and work on the monument stopped. Twenty-five years later, Congress appropriated some new money, and the monument was completed on 6 December 1884 at a total cost of $1.2 million. Many of the stones of the monument, which was designed by Robert Mills, were cut and polished at the plant of Matthew G. Emery, the last mayor of the City of Washington.

There is a total of 193 memorial stones on 31 of the 50 landings in the monument. Many were donated by cities, states, individuals, and citizens' groups (including quite a few Masonic Lodges). Others were donated by organizations outside the United States, including some with foreign inscriptions—such as those from Turkey, Bremen (Germany), Japan, Greece, Wales, and China.

Pope Pius IX donated a stone of African marble taken from a Roman Temple; it bore the inscription "Rome to America." In March 1854, during a period of anti-Catholic sentiment, the stone was stolen, and it is thought that it was thrown into the Potomac River. Although a reward was offered, the stone has never been found.

◄ *Work stopped in 1853, when the shaft was 152 feet high.* (Courtesy Library of Congress.)

John Adams

CHRONOLOGICAL EVENTS

30 October 1735	Born, Braintree (now Quincy), Massachusetts
16 July 1755	Graduated from Harvard College, Cambridge, Massachusetts
6 November 1758	Admitted to bar, Boston, Massachusetts
September 1765	Denounced Stamp Act
7 September 1770	Successfully defended Captain Thomas Preston, British officer involved in the Boston Massacre
1773	Elected to Massachusetts House of Deputies
1774	Elected to First Continental Congress
1775	Elected to Second Continental Congress
14 June 1775	Nominated George Washington to serve as commander in chief of the Continental army
11 June 1776	Appointed to committee to write Declaration of Independence
2 August 1776	Signed Declaration of Independence
1778	Served as a joint commissioner to France with Benjamin Franklin and Arthur Lee
August 1779	Drafted Massachusetts Constitution
1780	Appointed U.S. minister to the Netherlands
3 September 1783	Signed Treaty of Paris formally ending American Revolution
24 February 1785	Appointed U.S. minister to Great Britain
4 February 1789	Elected first vice president
13 February 1793	Reelected vice president
8 February 1796	Elected president
4 March 1797	Inaugurated president
3 April 1798	Submitted dispatches from commission to France to U.S. House of Representatives; known as the XYZ Affair
7 April 1798	Signed act establishing Mississippi Territory
June–July 1798	Signed Alien and Sedition Acts
7 May 1800	Signed act establishing Indiana Territory
1 November 1800	Took up residence in the White House
3 December 1800	Defeated for reelection as president
20 January 1801	Appointed John Marshall chief justice of Supreme Court
13 February 1801	Signed Judiciary Act
March 1801	Retired to Quincy, Massachusetts
4 July 1826	Died, Quincy, Massachusetts

BIOGRAPHY

EARLY LIFE. The second president of the United States, John Adams was born in Braintree, Massachusetts on 30 October 1735. Blessed with a keen intellect, Adams graduated from Harvard in 1755. He taught school briefly in Worcester, Massachusetts before he studied law under James Putnam. He was admitted to the Boston Bar on 6 November 1758 at the age of 23. Six years later, he married Abigail Smith, the daughter of a Congregational minister. In 1768, the Adamses moved from Braintree to Boston so that John could further his career as a lawyer.

Abigail Adams was one of the most important women in early America. (Courtesy National Archives.)

"Abigail Adams was a tiny woman, little more than five feet tall, with dark hair, piercing dark eyes, and a forceful personality that belied her size. Quiet and reserved as a child, she nonetheless displayed a brilliant mind and a fierce determination even then. As she matured, these qualities broke through her quiet exterior and she became voluble and outspoken, never afraid to assert her opinions whether in the company of friends, family, or heads of state.

To the modern observer, she is maddeningly contradictory. On the one hand, she was a fiery revolutionary, denouncing British tyranny in blistering rhetoric. She refused to be intimidated by the specter of British attack, even as she could hear the cannon and see the smoke of nearby battles; she raised four children, managed a farm, and conquered her intense feelings of loneliness and depression while her husband spent years away from her serving in the Continental Congress and negotiating with European powers. Her husband, John, called her a "heroine" for her courage, and indeed she was. Yet after the war she turned into a reactionary; she renounced all opposition to the new federal government as dangerous, blamed all political dissent on "foreign influence," and advocated the suppression of freedom of the press.

She was just as contradictory in other ways too. She argued for improved legal rights and education for women long before they became popular issues; but she always believed that a woman's place was in the home and, as she got older, became more and more obsessed with "delicacy" and moral purity in women. She professed to hate politics, and yet obviously thrived in her role as a politician's wife. Even in her relationships with her family, she displayed contradictory behavior. She tried to control the lives of everyone around her but instilled in her children a spirit of independence that made them resist—though not always successfully—her overwhelming influence. They often showed signs of resenting her interference in their lives, but they were also deeply attached to her. Despite her sometimes overbearing personality, she was a loving and generous woman. Her concern for her family and friends knew no bounds, and they, in turn, loved her unreservedly."

- *Lynne Withey,* Dearest Friend, A Life of Abigail Adams.

ADAMS AND THE REVOLUTIONARY MOVEMENT. Adams soon gained a reputation as a brilliant lawyer. He successfully defended the popular patriot merchant John Hancock against charges of smuggling. He also secured an acquittal for Captain Thomas Preston, a British officer charged, in part, with firing on American civilians in what became known as the Boston Massacre. An early and consistent champion of the patriot cause, Adams was soon rewarded with election to the Massachusetts House of Deputies as a representative from Boston. Adams quickly emerged as a principal and respected leader of the movement for independence in the state.

On 17 June 1774, Adams was chosen one of Massachusetts's delegates to the First Continental Congress. In 1775, Adams served in the Second Continental Congress as well. On both occasions, he and his cousin, Samuel Adams, established themselves as the most prominent leaders in the push for independence. John Adams worked tirelessly and patiently trying to convince moderates to give up their hope of compromise with Great Britain. He was, in part, responsible for the choice of George Washington as commander in chief, as well as for the selection of Thomas Jefferson to draft the Declaration of Independence. Most important of all, however, he was the principal agent behind the decision of the Continental Congress to declare independence on 2 July 1776.

Paul Revere's engraving of what came to be known as the Boston Massacre showed Captain Thomas Preston ordering his troops to fire on the crowd on 5 March 1770. Three Americans were killed, including Crispus Attucks, the first African American casualty. John Adams and Josiah Quincy were the only people who would defend the British soldiers. Adams proved that Preston did not give the order to fire on the civilians. (Courtesy National Archives.)

Samuel Adams was John Adams's cousin. He helped stir up the hatred of the British troops which eventually led to the Boston Massacre. This bust of him is by John Singleton Copley. (Courtesy National Archives.)

After U.S. independence had been declared, Adams served the new nation as a diplomat. Appointed to replace Silas Deane as commissioner to France, Adams departed for Paris on 13 February 1778. There he joined Benjamin Franklin, with whom he stayed. Although he lacked the charm and tact of Franklin, Adams brought much-needed discipline to the U.S. mission and put its correspondence and accounts in order. He also brought a healthy doubt of French motives to the deliberations. After carrying out his duties, he left for Massachusetts on 27 March 1779. Six months later he was chosen, along with Franklin and John Jay, to negotiate peace with Great Britain. Adams's presence proved so critical to the success of the treaty negotiations that he was subsequently appointed to serve as the U.S. minister to Great Britain from 1785 to 1788.

Adams's greatest contribution to the revolutionary cause, however, may have come from his pen. Adams emerged as one of the principal writers and most brilliant political thinkers of the revolutionary generation. As early as 1765, he published, in the Boston *Gazette*, his "Dissertation on the Canon and Feudal Law" opposing the recent acts of Parliament. In 1774, he published his famous "Novanglus" letters in response to the Tory writings of Daniel Leonard who wrote under the pen name "Massachusettensis." In 1776, he wrote the influential "Thoughts on Government" to answer what he

John Adams was sent to Paris to join Benjamin Franklin and Arthur Lee as a member of the commission to France. This painting shows Franklin at the French Court. (Courtesy National Archives.)

thought were the dangerously anarchic and democratic principles expressed in Thomas Paine's popular pamphlet "Common Sense." Chosen to represent Braintree at the Massachusetts constitutional convention in August 1779, Adams submitted a plan for a bicameral (two houses) legislature with a strong executive. This plan not only served as the framework of the state's new government but also was a model for the Federal Constitution of 1789. While in Europe, Adams wrote a three-volume *Defence of the Constitutions of the United States of America* in response to European criticisms of the new nation. In the 1780s, Adams emerged as one of the principal spokesmen on behalf of the need for a strong central government.

VICE PRESIDENT. Adams found his tenure as Washington's vice president extremely unpleasant. Holding what was largely a ceremonial office, Adams yearned for a position of responsibility and action. Nonetheless, he was hardly inactive during Washington's administration. He continually fought for titles and other means of elevating the principal executive offices of the new government in the eyes of the common people. In 1791, he published his famed "Discourses on Davila" in the *United States Gazette* in reaction to what he perceived as the excesses of the French Revolution. Adams also cast the tie-breaking vote in the U.S. Senate on more than 20 different occasions.

PRESIDENT. John Adams was the first president to serve for only one term. (His son, John Quincy Adams, more than 20 years later, would be the next). Some of his political difficulties can be attributed to his somewhat reserved and even pompous personality, but the bulk of his problem lay with the growing divisions among the American people and within the newly established government. The ongoing Anglo-French conflict continued to polarize Republicans and Federalists along increasingly sectional lines. Republicans and southerners favored the cause of France and feared the growth of the federal government at the expense of the states. On the other hand, Federalists and a major-

ity of northerners sided with their trade partners in Great Britain and sought to create a more powerful central government to combat what they felt was a growing sense of lawlessness among Americans. Even more troubling for Adams was the division within the Federalist ranks between himself and Alexander Hamilton, who questioned Adams's devotion to the party.

These divisions first became apparent in the presidential election of 1796. The Republicans chose Thomas Jefferson as their candidate and campaigned against the unpopular Jay's Treaty. The Federalists had settled on Adams as their presidential candidate, with Thomas Pinckney of South Carolina as the vice president. Since, at this time, each presidential elector had two votes, the Federalist plan was to have each Federalist elector cast one ballot for Adams and one for Pinckney. The U.S. House of Representative would then elevate Adams to the office of president. Hamilton, who feared that he could not control the independent-minded Adams, plotted to throw the election to Pinckney by convincing the electors from South Carolina to withhold some of their votes from Adams. When news of this scheme leaked to New England, many electors there scratched Pinckney off their ballots. The result was that Adams beat Jefferson by the slightest of margins, receiving 71 electoral votes to Jefferson's 68. The division within the Federalist Party had almost elected a Republican president. Equally troubling was the evidence of sectional divisions. Of the mere 18 electoral votes that Jefferson received in the northern states, all but 5 came from Pennsylvania. For his part, Adams received only two votes from the southern states in the Electoral College. The division within the Federalist ranks would continue to plague Adams's administration, particularly since he chose to retain Washington's cabinet officers, many of whom were loyal supporters of Alexander Hamilton.

FOREIGN RELATIONS. The presidential election of 1796 increased tensions between the United States and France. Angered by Jay's Treaty, the

Charles Cotesworth Pinckney was a member of the special mission to France in 1797. He refused to offer a bribe to French officials in the XYZ Affair. Pinckney was the Federalist nominee for vice president in 1800 and for president in 1804 and 1808. (Courtesy Library of Congress.)

French Directory had tried to influence the election on behalf of Jefferson and his Republican allies. The election of Adams confirmed the French Government in its hostility to the Federalist administration in the United States. Like Great Britain before them, France began seizing neutral U.S. shipping, and in December 1796, it rejected the embassy of the U.S. diplomat, Thomas Pinckney (brother of Charles Cotesworth Pinckney). Adams responded on 31 May 1797 by appointing a new diplomatic mission to Paris led by two Federalists, Charles Cotesworth Pinckney and John Marshall, and one Republican, Elbridge Gerry. They were instructed to negotiate a treaty of commerce and amity (friendship). The three diplomats arrived in Paris on 4 October 1797 and were unofficially entertained by the French minister, Charles Maurice de Talleyrand, four days later. Talleyrand delayed the beginning of official negotiations. On 18 October, the U.S. mission was visited by three of Talleyrand's aides, Hottinguer, Hauteval, and Bellamy (subsequently known as "X, Y, and Z"). Talleyrand's aides demanded, as a condition for opening negotiations, a public apology for some criticisms Adams had made against the French Government the previous spring, a loan of $12 million, and a bribe of $250,000 for Talleyrand and other members of the Directory. When the diplomats refused to meet these terms, Talleyrand denied them their passports and detained them in France (Gerry did not leave for the United States until July 1798). In April 1798, Adams presented the entire diplomatic correspondence to Congress, and it was published by the Senate. The "XYZ Affair," as it came to be known, became an issue that fueled anti-French and pro-war sentiment.

In the aftermath of the XYZ Affair, many Federalists favored an immediate declaration of war against France. Such a war would not only serve to defend U.S. honor and unite public opinion behind a patriotic cause but would also politically damage the pro-French Republican Party. Like Washington before him, however, Adams sought to avoid conflict with European powers at war, and he refused to ask for a declaration of war. He did, nonetheless, agree to prepare the nation for the possibility of war. From the end of March to the middle of July 1798, Congress passed a series of 20 acts providing for the national defense. Commerce with France was banned, and the 1778 treaties of mutual defense with France were officially suspended. The army was tripled in size and funds were allocated for the fortification of harbors. A new cabinet office, the Department of the Navy, was established and money was appropriated to complete construction of 3 frigates and to begin building 24 more. George Washington was to be placed in charge of the U.S. forces, with Alexander Hamilton as his second in command. The naval buildup proved particularly timely, for France began an undeclared naval war with the United States in November 1798. This "Quasi-War," as it has become known, lasted for almost two years. Although Adams's military buildup helped the U.S. Navy to force the French to the treaty table, the cost was higher taxes, which undermined the popularity of the Federalist Party.

DOMESTIC POLICY. Faced with an increased likelihood of full-scale war with France, the Federalist-led Congress sought to ensure the loyalty of the residents of the United States in the event of armed conflict. They also tried to attack the patriotism of pro-French Republicans and to decrease criticism of the Federalist administration and its policies. The so-called Alien and Sedition Acts were passed in the summer of 1798. They threatened the right to publish political dissent and ultimately proved extremely unpopular. The Alien Act was actually a series of three laws, the Naturalization Act, an Act Concerning Aliens, and an Act Respecting Alien Enemies, all passed between 18 June and 6 July 1798. The Naturalization Act increased the residency requirement for aliens seeking to become citizens from 5 years, as prescribed in an act of 1795, to 14 years. The purpose of this measure was to hinder the work of the leading Republican writers, many of whom were recent European refugees. The other

This engraving of President John Adams shows the seals of the 16 states then in the Union. The quote at the top refers to the French bribe requested from the U.S. commissioners in the XYZ Affair. (Courtesy Library of Congress.)

A STRONG NAVY

. . . With you, gentlemen, I sincerely hope that the final result of the negotiations now pending with France may prove as fortunate to our country as they have been commenced with sincerity and prosecuted with deliberation and caution. With you I cordially agree that so long as a predatory war is carried on against our commerce we should sacrifice the interests and disappoint the expectations of our constituents should we for a moment relax that system of maritime defense which has resulted in such beneficial effects. With you I confidently believe that few persons can be found within the United States who do not admit that a navy, well organized, must constitute the natural and efficient defense of this country against all foreign hostility.

Those who recollect the distress and danger to this country in former periods from the want of arms must exult in the assurance from their Representatives that we shall soon rival foreign countries not only in the number but in the quality of arms completed from our own manufactories.

With you, gentlemen, I fully agree that the great increase of revenue is a proof that the measures of maritime defense were founded in wisdom. This policy has raised us in the esteem of foreign nations. That national spirit and those latent energies which had not been and are not yet fully known to any were not entirely forgotten by those who had lived long enough to see in former times their operation and some of their effects. Our fellow-citizens were undoubtedly prepared to meet every event which national honor or national security could render necessary. These, it is to be hoped, are secured at the cheapest and easiest rate; if not, they will be secured at more expense. . . .

- *In 1798 and in 1799, Congress voted huge sums of money to expand the armed forces as an undeclared naval war with France increased tensions between the two nations. U.S. ships, operating mainly in the Caribbean, captured almost 100 French vessels while suffering serious losses themselves. In this letter, dated 27 November 1800, President Adams reaffirms his belief that a strong navy is essential to U.S. national security.*

  In the early years of the nation, the president's legislative proposals, recommendations, and observations came in formal letters addressed to a branch of Congress—either to the House of Representatives or to the Senate. Today, a member of the president's political party in Congress usually performs this function by introducing the appropriate legislation stating that it has the endorsement—or support—of the president.

two acts authorized the president to deport any alien believed to present a danger to the security of the nation or suspected of "treasonable or secret" leanings and to arrest or imprison citizens of an enemy power during wartime.

Far more controversial was the Act for the Punishment of Certain Crimes. Passed on 14 July 1798, the Sedition Act, as it was popularly known, made it a crime for citizens to organize in opposition to the execution of national laws, resist any federal officer, or aid "any insurrection, riot, unlawful assembly, or combination." The act further provided for a maximum sentence of two years in prison and a $2,000 fine for the publication of "any false, scandalous and malicious writing" that questioned the reputation of the president and the government of the United States. The enforcement of this act by the Federalists was extremely one-sided. All 10 men convicted of seditious libel during Adams's administration were Republicans. Not a single charge was raised against any of the Federalist writers, despite the fact that they regularly heaped slander and abuse upon Vice President Thomas Jefferson. The act also provided additional evidence of the growing sectional divide in the nation, for it passed through Congress with only two southern votes in support.

In the eyes of the Republican opposition, the Alien and Sedition Acts not only threatened Americans' right to free speech; they also violated the Constitution by giving the federal courts powers not explicitly authorized by that document. This view was given public expression in a series of resolutions passed by the state legislatures of Virginia and Kentucky in late 1798. The Virginia and Kentucky Resolutions, written by James Madison and Thomas Jefferson respectively, argued that the U.S. Constitution was a compact between sovereign states and that the Alien and Sedition Acts had violated that compact's terms. They further claimed that under such circumstances the individual states could judge the offensive acts unconstitutional and were "in duty bound to interpose for arresting the progress of the evil." After seven northern states objected that only the Supreme Court had the authority to judge the constitutionality of federal law, the Kentucky legislature responded with another set of resolves on 22 November 1799. These insisted on the states' right to "nullify" unconstitutional acts of the federal government. Although the controversy proved short-lived—all of the Alien and Sedition Acts either expired or were repealed shortly after Jefferson's election in 1800—the interrelated issues of states' rights and nullification continued to disrupt the United States intermittently in the period before the Civil War.

Despite the unpopularity of the Alien and Sedition Acts and the high taxes imposed to pay for the expansion of the U.S. military, Hamilton's supporters in the Federalist Party still hoped that the onset of war with France would carry them to political victory over their Republican opponents. They were bitterly disappointed in early 1789 when, without any prior warning, Adams nomi-

nated William Vans Murray as minister to France. Despite the opposition of many leading members of his party—the Federalists in the Senate agreed to the mission only after Adams threatened to resign the presidency to Thomas Jefferson. A delegation of Murray, W. R. Davie of North Carolina, and Chief Justice Oliver Ellsworth, left for France in November 1799. They were instructed to secure compensation for French assaults on U.S. shipping, as well as the release of the United States from the pledges of mutual defense that were made in the Treaties of 1778. Signed on 30 September 1800, the Treaty of Morfontaine, like Jay's Treaty before it, fell far short of expectations. The agreement, commonly known as the Convention of 1800, released the United States from its obligation to defend France but left the issue of French compensation for U.S. shipping unresolved.

Despite its shortcomings, the Convention ended the costly and increasingly unpopular Quasi-War with France and paved the way for the Louisiana Purchase some three years later. Adams's dogged and independent pursuit of peace, however, had prompted an irreparable split within the Federalist Party. Hamilton publicized his dissatisfaction with the President among the leaders of the party in his "Letter from Alexander Hamilton concerning the Public Conduct and Character of John Adams." For his part, Adams finally demanded the resignation of several cabinet officers who were known to be more loyal to Hamilton than to himself. Dispirited and divided, the Federalist Party finally gave way to the Republican opposition when Thomas Jefferson defeated John Adams in the presidential election of 1800.

Before leaving office, however, Adams left one last Federalist legacy for the young nation. On 13 February 1801, three weeks before Jefferson's inauguration, the outgoing Federalist Congress passed a Judiciary Act that reorganized the federal court system, extended its scope, and created 23 new judicial offices. Many of Adams's judicial appointments (known as the "midnight judges" because Adams signed their commissions the night

A PROCLAMATION

Whereas an act of the Congress of the United States was passed on the 9th day of February, 1793, entitled "An act regulating foreign coins, and for other purposes," in which it was enacted "that foreign gold and silver coins shall pass current as money within the United States and be a legal tender for the payment of all debts and demands" at the several and respective rates therein stated; and that "at the expiration of three years next ensuing the time when the coinage of gold and silver agreeably to the act [entitled] "An act establishing a mint and regulating the coins of the United States" shall commence at the Mint of the United States (which time shall be announced by the proclamation of the President of the United Sates), all foreign gold coins and all foreign silver coins, except Spanish milled dollars and parts of such dollars, shall cease to be a legal tender as aforesaid:

Now, therefore, I, the said John Adams, President of the United States, hereby proclaim, announce, and give notice to all whom it may concern that, agreeably to the act last above mentioned, the coinage of silver at the Mint of the United States commenced on the 15th day of October, 1794, and the coinage of gold on the 31st day of July, 1795; and that consequently, in conformity to the act first above mentioned, all foreign silver coins, except Spanish milled dollars and parts of such dollars, will cease to pass current as money within the United States and to be a legal tender for the payment of any debts or demands after the 15th day of October next, and all foreign gold coins will cease to pass current as money within the United States and to be a legal tender as aforesaid for the payment of any debts or demands after the 31st day of July, which will be A.D. 1798.

• *After the American Revolution ended (1781) but before the adoption of the Constitution of the United States (1789), the lack of a uniform national currency worked hardships on U.S. merchants. Imports of foreign goods drained the new nation of gold and silver. Paper currency, with its constant fluctuations in value, was hated by most businessmen.*

Today, we accept paper currency because of our faith in the U.S. Government. At this time, paper money had to be backed by either gold or silver. Counterfeiters, however, created doubt in the value of paper currency. Also, many state governments just printed money to pay debts. Revolutionary soldiers, for example, often sold their paper wage certificates at one-eight of their face value— "face value" is the worth printed on money. In Rhode Island, the state legislature passed a law providing for a juryless trial before judges of anyone who refused to accept paper money at the value printed on it (1785). Many creditors fled the state to avoid having to accept this almost worthless currency.

The Constitution of the United States gives Congress the power "to coin Money, regulate the value thereof, and of foreign Coin." In 1792, Congress established the United States coinage system. President John Adams announced that only American gold and silver coins would be legal as of 31 July 1798. Spanish "milled dollars and parts of such dollars" were exempt. (In coinage, a "mill" refers to a raised or grooved edge. This prevented clipping off a piece of the gold or silver coin and melting it for further use, thus debasing or reducing the true value of the coin.) Since Spain controlled the area west of the Mississippi River, Spanish coins circulated in the United States between the Appalachian Mountains and the Mississippi River.

Adams's Proclamation summarizes monetary (economic) history during the first years of the nation.

At age 89, John Adams saw his son, John Quincy Adams, elected president of the United States. (Courtesy National Archives.)

before he left office) had long and distinguished careers in the federal courts, and profoundly influenced the development of U.S. law and constitutional theory. Perhaps his most famous and brilliant appointment was that of the Virginia Federalist John Marshall, whose tenure as chief justice is among the most important and renowned in the history of the U.S. Supreme Court.

RETIREMENT. Upon leaving the presidency, John Adams retired to his farm in Braintree, Massachusetts. From there, he took great pleasure in the rising political career of his son, John Quincy Adams. He also resumed his correspondence and rekindled his friendship with his one-time political opponent, Thomas Jefferson. In the closing years of their lives, each gained a renewed appreciation of the other. Remarkably, they died on the same day, 4 July 1826. Fittingly, the two men who had done so much to achieve America's independence both died on the very day devoted to commemorating it.

VICE PRESIDENT

Thomas Jefferson
(1743–1826)

CHRONOLOGICAL EVENTS

1743	Born, Shadwell, Virginia, 13 April
1769	Elected to Virginia House of Burgesses
1775	Elected to Second Continental Congress
1776	Wrote Declaration of Independence
1779	Elected governor of Virginia
1785	Appointed U.S. minister to France
1789	Appointed secretary of state
1796	Elected vice president
1800	Elected president
1826	Died, near Charlottesville, Virginia, 4 July

BIOGRAPHY

A tall, red-haired lawyer and legislator from Virginia, Thomas Jefferson was only 33 years old when he drafted the Declaration of Independence. Its affirmation of human equality made Jefferson the philosopher of the American Revolution. After serving as wartime governor of Virginia, Jefferson went abroad as U.S. minister to France.

President George Washington appointed Jefferson the first secretary of state. In the cabinet, he opposed Treasury Secretary Alexander Hamilton's plans for a strong central government to promote U.S. industries. Jefferson advocated a more limited government and an agrarian democracy.

The first contested presidential election was caused by Washington's decision not to run for a third term in 1796. The Federalist Party put forward Vice President John Adams for president. The opposition party (called Republicans or Democratic-Republicans) supported Jefferson.

Since Jefferson's strength lay in the South, where Adams was the weakest, the Federalists chose Thomas Pinckney of South Carolina for vice president. Adams narrowly won, but some New England Federalists voted against Pinckney in the Electoral College. Since Jefferson received the second largest number of electoral ballots, he became vice president. In 1804, the Twelfth Amendment was passed. It required electors to vote separately for presidential and vice presidential candidates.

Once a friend of Adams, Jefferson disagreed with Adams's Federalist policies and played no role in his administration. He believed that the vice presidency was really a legislative post. Yet he was also out of step with the Federalist majority in the U. S. Senate. Congressional passage of the Alien and Sedition Acts in 1798 deeply offended Jefferson. In response, he anonymously authored the Kentucky Resolutions, which argued that states could nullify federal laws they considered unconstitutional.

Jefferson devoted much of his four years as vice president to compiling the first manual of parliamentary procedure published in the United States. The relatively light duties of presiding over Senate debates also gave him time to organize the opposition Republican Party. In 1800, Jefferson ran as the Republican candidate for president and defeated Adams. Years later, when they were both former presidents, they resumed their correspondence and a friendship forged during the Revolution.

THE CABINET

SECRETARY OF STATE
Timothy Pickering, 1797
John Marshall, 1800

SECRETARY OF WAR
James McHenry, 1797
Benjamin Stoddert, 1800
Samuel Dexter, 1801

SECRETARY OF THE TREASURY
Oliver Wolcott, Jr., 1797
Samuel Dexter, 1801

POSTMASTER GENERAL
Joseph Habersham, 1797

ATTORNEY GENERAL
Charles Lee, 1797

SECRETARY OF THE NAVY[1]
Benjamin Stoddert, 1798

1. Navy Department established 30 April 1798.

(Courtesy Library of Congress.)

John Marshall (1755–1835). Marshall was appointed secretary of state by President John Adams in 1800. He had previously declined Adams's invitation to serve as secretary of war.

As secretary of state, Marshall reaffirmed the U.S. position on neutral rights at sea and argued against war with France.

Adams nominated Marshall for the post of chief justice of the Supreme Court in January 1801. He took his seat on 4 February. He continued as secretary of state until the end of the Adams administration although he did not draw the salary of that office.

Marshall was one of the most influential chief justices of the U.S. Supreme Court. He established the precedent of judicial review of state court decisions and the right of the Court to declare acts of Congress unconstitutional (*Marbury v. Madison,* 1803). He upheld the implied powers of the Constitution and, therefore, the right of Congress to charter the Bank of the United States in *McCulloch v. Maryland* (1819). Marshall served as chief justice until his death in 1835.

John Adams stated, "My gift of John Marshall to the people of the United States was the proudest act of my life."

FAMILY

CHRONOLOGICAL EVENTS

23 November 1744	Abigail Smith born	29 May 1770	Son, Charles, born
25 October 1764	Abigail Smith married John Adams	15 September 1772	Son, Thomas Boylston, born
		30 November 1800	Son, Charles, died
14 July 1765	Daughter, Abigail (Nabby), born	13 August 1813	Daughter, Abigail, died
		28 October 1818	Abigail Adams died
11 July 1767	Son, John Quincy, born	4 July 1826	John Adams died

(Courtesy Library of Congress).

The only female Adams who has had anything like her due from historians is John's wife, Abigail (1744–1818). Still, despite the fact that she was one of the brightest, most public-minded, and most sacrificing of the family, she has been treated as little more than a mirror for her husband and the age. The entry for her in the concise edition of the authoritative *Dictionary of American Biography* sums her up in the single phrase: "Wrote distinguished letters containing vivid pictures of the times." Her personal contribution, and her essential part in the careers of her husband John and her eldest son John Quincy, have not yet had the spotlight.

• Jack Shepherd, *The Adams Chronicles: Four Generations of Greatness.*

Abigail Smith was 19 years old when she married John Adams in her parents' home in Weymouth, Massachusetts. She was a granddaughter of the distinguished Massachusetts legislator Colonel John Quincy, and her mother was concerned that she would waste her life on a country lawyer.

They were married for 54 years. She was a strong and loyal partner to her husband, and they had four children live to adulthood: Abigail (Nabby), John Quincy, Charles, and Thomas Boylston. Nabby married William Smith, a former

officer and her father's secretary. President Adams appointed him surveyor of the Port of New York. He later served in U.S. the House of Representatives.

Charles died an alcoholic when he was 30. Thomas Boylston also drank heavily and died in debt. John Quincy went to Europe with his father in 1778. President George Washington appointed him minister to The Hague, beginning a long and distinguished career.

When Charles died, Abigail and John took his daughter, Caroline, to live with them. When Nabby died, they also raised her daughter, Susan.

ADAMS NATIONAL HISTORIC SITE

135 Adams Street
P.O. Box 531
Quincy, Massachusetts 02269-0531
Tel: (617) 770-1175

The John Adams Birthplace is located only 75 feet from the John Quincy Adams Birthplace. They are the oldest surviving presidential birthplaces in the United States.
(Courtesy National Park Service, Adams National Historic site.)

Located approximately eight miles south of Boston. Can be reached via Interstate 93 (Southeast Expressway), Exit 8. Open daily, 19 April through 10 November, from 9 A.M. to 5 P.M. Admission fee, with discounts available for educational groups. Call in advance for fee waiver. Children ages 16 and under admitted free. There are 11 historic structures on 12 acres. Four of these structures are open for tours: The John Adams and John Quincy Adams birthplaces, the Old House, and the United First Parish Church. Handicapped accessible, with the exception of the second floor of the Old House. Trolley service links the visitor center (1250 Hancock Street) with the birthplaces and the Old House. Administered by the National Park Service, U.S. Department of the Interior.

The John Adams Birthplace is located at 133 Franklin Street. It was built by Joseph Penniman in 1681 and remained in the Penniman family until 1720. At that time Adams's father, Deacon John, purchased the house and six acres of property. John Adams was born in this home on 30 October 1735. In 1744, his father purchased the house across from the birthplace property. Upon his death in 1761, John inherited that house (now known as the John Quincy Adams Birthplace). His brother, Peter Boylston Adams, inherited the original homestead. In 1774, John purchased the birthplace home from his brother.

The John Quincy Adams Birthplace is located at 141 Franklin Street. Built by Samuel Belcher in 1663, it remained in the Belcher family until John Adams's father purchased it in 1744. In 1761, John Adams inherited the house upon the death of his father. He married Abigail Smith on 25 October 1764, and on 11 July 1767, their second child, John Quincy, was born. In 1787, while John was serving as U.S. minister to Great Britain, the Adamses purchased the house which stands at 135 Adams Street. In 1788, they returned home from England to their new residence and did not reside in John Quincy's birthplace home again. John Quincy and his wife, Louisa Catherine, resided in his own birthplace home during the summers of 1806 through 1808.

Successive Adams family members continued to own the two birthplace homes and rent them to tenants until 1893. The sites were shown as house museums by the Quincy Historical Society between 1893 and 1940, when the Adams family donated them to the city of Quincy. The sites were presented to the American people on 1 May 1979 by the city of Quincy, in cooperation with the Adams Memorial Society. The homes are part of the Adams National Historic Site.

The Old House is located at 135 Adams Street. It was built by Leonard Vassall, a sugar-planter from Jamaica, in 1730. Vassall's daughter, Anna, inherited the house before marrying John Borland, a British loyalist. They fled the country during the American Revolution, but after the war, Anna recovered the house and sold it to her son, Leonard Vassall Borland. In 1787, John Adams, while he was still at his diplomatic post in London, purchased the house from Borland.

Adams named the homestead Peacefield, in honor of the peace he had helped to create in 1784 with the Treaty of Paris. During Adams's presidency, Abigail made several improvements, including the

▲ *The Old House contains priceless heirlooms and Colonial furnishings that belonged to four successive generations of the Adams family.*
(Courtesy National Park Service, Adams National Historic Site.)

addition of the east wing and a front porch. After his retirement from the presidency in 1801, Adams returned to Peacefield and lived there until his death in 1826.

Upon Adams's death, his son, John Quincy, inherited the house. In 1836, he added a passageway connecting the kitchen wing and the east wing at the back of the house. It became known as the President's Walk because he used this passageway to walk to his study without traveling downstairs or through the guest room. He lived there until his death in 1848. John Quincy's son, Charles Francis, inherited the house in 1852. The house became the summer home for the third generation of the Adams family. It was this generation that called it the Old House, because Charles Francis had built a new house nearby.

Following the deaths of Charles Francis (1886) and his wife, Abigail (1889), their youngest son, Brooks, assumed occupancy and care of the Old House. Brooks dedicated his time to preserving it, and he arranged that the house would become a museum after his death (1927). The Adams Memorial Society then took custody of the property, maintaining it until 1946, when the property was designated a National Historic Site and the Adams family dedicated the property to the American people.

▲ *John Adams was buried beside his wife, Abigail, at the Congregational Church in Quincy, Massachusetts.*
(Courtesy Library of Congress.)

Thomas Jefferson

CHRONOLOGICAL EVENTS

13 April 1743	Born at Shadwell plantation, Goochland, (Albemarle County), Virginia
5 April 1767	Admitted to bar, Williamsburg, Virginia
11 May 1769	Elected to Virginia House of Burgesses
1774	Wrote *A Summary View of the Rights of British America*
25 March 1775	Selected as Virginia delegate to Second Continental Congress
June–July 1776	Wrote Declaration of Independence
2 August 1776	Signed Declaration of Independence
7 October 1776	Elected to Virginia House of Delegates
1 June 1779	Elected governor of Virginia
1779	Wrote Virginia Statute for Religious Freedom
1780	Reelected governor of Virginia
6 June 1783	Elected to First Congress
1785	Published *Notes on the State of Virginia*
2 May 1785	Appointed U.S. minister to France
1789	Appointed secretary of state
1791	Joined with James Madison in opposition to Alexander Hamilton's program for a national bank
31 July 1793	Resigned as secretary of state
8 February 1797	Elected vice president
1798	Wrote Kentucky Resolutions
11 February 1800	Tied with Burr in presidential voting in U.S. House of Representatives
17 February 1800	Elected president
4 March 1801	Inaugurated president
January 1803	Approved Louisiana Purchase
January 1803	Commissioned Lewis and Clark Expedition
1804	Reelected president
4 March 1805	Inaugurated president
22 December 1807	Signed Embargo Act
9 January 1808	Signed second Embargo Act
1 March 1809	Signed Nonintercourse Act
4 March 1809	Retired to Monticello estate, Virginia
1819	Led effort to establish the University of Virginia
4 July 1826	Died at Monticello, near Charlottesville, Virginia

BIOGRAPHY

EARLY LIFE. Thomas Jefferson was born at Shadwell, a small plantation in Albemarle County, Virginia, on 13 April 1743. His father was a moderately prosperous farmer and surveyor who served in the House of Burgesses. He died when Jefferson was 14 years old. Peter Jefferson not only left his oldest son about 5,000 acres of farmland but also the responsibilities of a "gentleman freeholder" that young Jefferson quickly assumed. His mother, Jane Randolph, was a member of one of the most important families in Virginia.

From age 14 to age 16, Jefferson was taught by the Reverend James Maury who was also the teacher of James Madison and James Monroe. When he was 17 years old, Jefferson enrolled at the College of William and Mary. There he met Francis Fauquier, the governor of Virginia and George Wythe, a dedicated law professor. Jefferson studied law with Wythe and was admitted to the bar in 1767.

A law career had little appeal for Jefferson. He became a member of the colonial legislature, married Martha Wayles Skelton, and spent most of his time as a planter, running his plantation at Monticello. At the death of his father-in-law, John Wayles, Jefferson's land holdings doubled. John Wayles's death also left Jefferson with a large debt. Despite his lands and ownership of nearly 200 slaves, Jefferson wrestled with debt for the rest of his life.

HOUSE OF BURGESSES. Jefferson served in the Virginia House of Burgesses as the delegate from Albemarle County from 1769 to 1774. He steadily opposed regulations and taxes passed by the British Parliament. As tension between Great Britain and its colonies increased, he wrote *A Summary View of the Rights of British America* (1774). The pamphlet contained a ringing sentence— "The whole art of government consists in the art of being honest" —that drew attention to Jefferson's abilities as a writer. Addressed to King George III as a petition on behalf of the American colonies, the pamphlet stated that Parliament had no rights over the colonies. Its publication placed

"Jefferson delivered his first attack in print upon slavery in 1774, when he published a pamphlet entitled *A Summary View of the Rights of British America.* Intended to serve as a policy guide to the Virginia House of Burgesses in its controversy with the British Government, *A Summary View* took the radical ground that Americans owed no allegiance whatever to the British Parliament, a position not assumed by the Continental Congress until 1775. Although Jefferson's handiwork was rejected by the House of Burgesses, it helped create a favorable opinion of his literary ability and called attention to his advanced views in the matter of colonial rights. Had it not been for the publication of *A Summary View,* it is unlikely that Jefferson would have been designated in June 1776 to write the Declaration of Independence."

• *John Chester Miller,* The Wolf by the Ears.

Jefferson in the forefront of those who defied Parliament's efforts to control the colonies. Americans had no wish to separate from Great Britain, Jefferson wrote, but the solution rested with Parliament: "Let them name their terms, but let them be just." In Great Britain, the plea was rejected with scorn.

DECLARATION OF INDEPENDENCE. Jefferson was selected as a delegate to the Second Continental Congress in 1775. He acquired a reputation as a revolutionary radical as well as a skilled writer and was appointed to the committee responsible for drafting a declaration of independence for the new nation. The other members of the committee—John Adams, Benjamin Franklin, Roger Sherman, and Robert R. Livingston—chose him to write it. Although the final draft of Jefferson's Declaration of Independence was toned down by the committee, its main features

▲ *"Signers of the Declaration of Independence" was painted by John Trumbull in 1817. The painting hangs in the Rotunda of the U.S. Capitol. It shows the drafting committee submitting the Declaration of Independence to the Second Continental Congress. The men standing at the table are, (left to right): John Adams, Roger Sherman, Robert R. Livingston, Thomas Jefferson, and Benjamin Franklin.* (Courtesy Architect of the Capitol.)

▲ *The Declaration of Independence was read publicly for the first time at noon on 8 July 1776 in Philadelphia, Pennsylvania. The bell in the State House, now Independence Hall, rang after the official reading. On 4 July 1826, the Liberty Bell rang to celebrate the 50th anniversary of independence. Thomas Jefferson and John Adams died within hours of each other on that day.*
(Courtesy National Archives.)

PREAMBLE

When, in the course of human events, it becomes necessary for one people to dissolve the political bands which have connected them with another, and to assume, among the powers of the earth, the separate and equal station to which the laws of nature and of nature's God entitle them, a decent respect to the opinions of mankind requires that they should declare the causes which impel them to the separation.

• *Thomas Jefferson wrote the Declaration of Independence in rented rooms near the State House in Philadelphia. This is the Preamble or introduction to that document.*

remained, particularly its emphasis on government by popular consent and the "inalienable" rights of all men to "life, liberty, and the pursuit of happiness." Jefferson's literary skills were at their peak when he wrote this document. It continues to be the clearest expression of the goals of both the American Revolution and the American people.

SLAVERY. Although Jefferson hated slavery, he kept hundreds of slaves during his life, and he freed fewer than a dozen when he died. In his autobiography, written in 1821, Jefferson recalled that when he served in the colonial legislature he tried to do something about slavery, and failed: "I made one effort in that body for the permission of the emancipation of slaves, which was rejected: and indeed, during the regal government, nothing liberal could expect success." British merchants who controlled Parliament had vast investments in the slave trade, as Jefferson well knew, and he thought that their influence kept the slave trade open. The threat of a royal veto of a colonial slave law, Jefferson insisted, closed the last door to every hope of making things better for the slaves. But neither had slavery been outlawed by the new

nation after its independence had been won. Jefferson suffered the dilemma of a slaveowner who hated slavery but depended on slave labor. Mainly because of his large debt, he could never resolve that dilemma. Jefferson was always land-rich and cash-poor, even when the paper value of his slave holdings probably exceeded $60,000.

In 1820 Jefferson wrote, "We have the wolf by the ears; and we can neither hold him, nor safely let him go. Justice is in one scale, and self-preservation in the other." He felt that the issue was too controversial to be settled by passage of a law that many Southerners despised. He worried that the problem of slavery would someday tear apart the Union unless it was resolved.

A BUSY LAWMAKER. Jefferson was a member of the Virginia House of Delegates from 1776 to 1779, and he served two terms as governor of Virginia (1779–1781). As a member of the House of Delegates, he undertook the revision of Virginia's legal code, writing 126 bills, including the Virginia act "for Establishing Religious Freedom" that forbade the state from interfering in religious practices. Passed in 1785, after Jefferson had left office, the religious freedom law was hailed and imitated in most other states and in the enlightened parts of Western Europe as a milestone in human history.

Toward the end of the Revolutionary War, Jefferson began replying to some questions asked by a French diplomat concerning conditions in Virginia. Eventually, Jefferson published his lengthy answers as *Notes on the State of Virginia* (1785). The book rejected the notion that both European animal species and European ideas were far superior to their American counterparts. In these notes, Jefferson also took pains to point to the *Virginia Declaration of Rights* of 1776, which "declared it to be a truth, and a natural right, that the exercise of religion should be free." Later that year (1785), the Virginia legislature revoked all laws providing for a subsidized church, compulsory church attendance, and penalties for persons who questioned organized religion. "Statutory

Thomas Jefferson posed for the bust by Jean-Antoine Houdon while he was U.S. minister to France. Four years earlier, Jefferson had brought Houdon to the United States to prepare a statue of George Washington. The statue of Jefferson is now in the Boston Museum of the Fine Arts. (Courtesy National Archives.)

oppressions in religion being thus wiped away," Jefferson added, "we remain at present under those only imposed by the common law, or by our own acts of assembly." Jefferson wavered on slavery, but on the matter of religious freedom, he stood as firmly for total separation of church and state as any person in history.

While Jefferson was working on this book, his wife, Martha, died in September 1782. A widower with three daughters, Jefferson plunged back into public service. Sent back to the Congress in 1783, he was active in preparing a report that established the dollar with a coinage based on the decimal system as the national currency.

U.S. MINISTER TO FRANCE. Jefferson was appointed by Congress as Benjamin Franklin's successor as minister to France. He took up his duties in Paris late in 1785 and became a witness to the rebellion that would in time bring down the Bourbon king, Louis XVI. The French Revolution ended the medieval society that still sharply divided European society into the few "haves" and the many "have-nots." Jefferson believed that the French Revolution, like the American Revolution, would result in a republican form of government as a model for other European powers.

Before he left Europe in 1789, Jefferson made several trips that helped broaden his ideas on government, science, and architecture. In London, Jefferson was snubbed by George III at the English Court. English aristocrats warned him that America would soon fail as an independent nation and then seek readmission into the British empire. He never forgot the snub or the warning. He also noted the terrible poverty of the common people in Europe and came to believe that it was in part caused by the close ties between the churches and the various governments.

While still in France, Jefferson had written to James Madison about his concern that one generation could make laws and commitments that would bind succeeding generations. "The earth belongs always to the living generation," Jefferson wrote. He expressed doubt about the wisdom and justice of incurring a heavy public debt that would have to be passed on to citizens who had not yet been born when the commitment was made. Jefferson figured that a generation lasted about 19 years, and he thought that constitutions and laws ought to be changed for each generation to prevent unjust burdens. The concept was typical of Jefferson's belief in change for the public good. However, as Madison pointed out, it ignored the many useful things created by each generation that involve long-term financing: roads, bridges, public buildings, and waterways.

SECRETARY OF STATE. Jefferson took leave from his diplomatic post in 1789, thinking he would return to Paris after a visit to Virginia. The new government created by the Constitutional Convention (Federal Convention) of 1787, where the Constitution was written, came into being in April 1789, and President George Washington asked Jefferson to serve in his cabinet as the first secretary of state. Jefferson took the post, realizing that he would become one of the President's most intimate advisers. Jefferson had followed closely the creation of the Constitution and had applauded the final draft with enthusiasm. His only criticism of any substance was a regret that the document did not contain a bill of rights. Jefferson encouraged his close friend James Madison to prepare a bill of rights for quick enactment. By the fall of 1789, Madison had moved Congress into sending 12 amendments to the states for ratification. As secretary of state, Jefferson proclaimed

the first 10 amendments ratified, and they were added to the Constitution on 10 December 1791. They became known as the Bill of Rights.

As secretary of state, Jefferson tried to keep the United States neutral as Napoleon's army swept across Europe. Great Britain responded to Napoleon's advances by blockading the continent. U.S. ships were seized on the high seas by both France and Great Britain, but the United States lacked the naval power to resist such violations of its neutrality.

BANK OF THE UNITED STATES. In domestic affairs, Jefferson was alarmed at Secretary of the Treasury Alexander Hamilton's proposal for a national bank. Hamilton's proposed Bank of the United States was part of a grand scheme to establish the credit of the government along British lines. Hamilton wanted Congress to pass the assumption bill under which the new federal government would assume the wartime debts of the states and thus create a national debt, with securities to be issued bearing the full faith and credit of the new federal government. This debt such as treasury notes and U.S. bonds would become part of a financial system that would be guaranteed by a stable lending agency, the federal government itself. The new national bank would make lending and commercial transactions flow smoothly, far preferable in Hamilton's eyes to an awkward arrangement of shaky banks chartered by the states.

Learning that compromises must be made to achieve great ends, Jefferson finally agreed to Hamilton's assumption bill in return for Hamilton's acceptance of legislation which would locate the federal capital on the banks of the Potomac River. President Washington traveled a few miles from his home at Mount Vernon to pick the actual spot where surveyors carved out a 10-square-mile location for the District of Columbia. Jefferson, a self-taught architect, anonymously drafted a plan for the presidential mansion, but his design was rejected. Meanwhile, Jefferson's plan for a state capitol building in Richmond was hurried to completion.

TO THE PRESIDENT OF THE UNITED STATES,

. . . If my own justification, or the interests of the republic shall require it, I reserve to myself the right of then appealing to my country, subscribing my name to whatever I write, and using with freedom and truth the facts and names necessary to place the cause in its just form before the tribunal. To a thorough disregard of the honors and emoluments of the office, I join as great a value for the esteem of my countrymen, and conscious of having merited it by an integrity which cannot be reproached, and by an enthusiastic devotion to their rights and liberty, I will not suffer my retirement to be clouded by the slanders of a man whose history, from the moment at which history can stoop to notice him, is a tissue of machinations against the liberty of the country which has not only received and given him bread, but heaped its honors on his head. . . . Though little known to the people of America, I believe, that as far as I am known, it is not as an enemy to the Republic, nor an intriguer against it, nor a waster of its revenue, nor prostitutor of it to the purposes of corruption, as the "American" represents me; and I confide that yourself are satisfied that as to the dissensions in the newspapers, not a syllable of them has ever proceeded from me, and that no cabals or intrigues of mine have produced those in the Legislature, and I hope I may promise both to you and myself, that none will receive aliment from me during the short space I have to remain in office, which will find ample employment in closing the present business of the department.

- *Thomas Jefferson wrote this letter to President George Washington on 9 September 1792. He was saying that he would not make his disagreements with Hamilton public while he was still in office, unless he felt that he had to defend his own reputation. The literal meaning of aliment is food, but Jefferson uses the word to refer to information.*

Jefferson later had doubts about his acceptance of Hamilton's plan for a national bank and decided that Hamilton's bank plan stretched the Constitution too far. When Washington asked him for an opinion, Jefferson opposed the assumption bill in strong language. After much thought, Washington decided to ignore Jefferson's advice and encouraged Hamilton's plans by signing the bank bill into law. Jefferson was fearful that many of Hamilton's supporters were too pro-British. He called them "monarchists," believers in a king. When Washington asked him to moderate his criticism, Jefferson resigned. He told Washington that Hamilton had "duped" (tricked) him into accepting the trade-off on the assumption and capital bills and called Hamilton's schemes "a tissue of machinations against the liberty of the country." Jefferson was also convinced that Hamilton was

trying to reshape foreign policy to harm the French and make the United States bow down to Great Britain in the process. On 1 January 1794, Jefferson resigned his position and became a private citizen.

For a few years Jefferson spent most of his time remodeling Monticello and trying to reduce his debts. He sold off some land and built a nail factory. Jefferson was furious when Hamilton pushed for ratification of the controversial Jay's Treaty (1794–1795). Jefferson thought that the treaty was an uneven series of concessions to Great Britain on all the troublesome issues such as trade and tariffs. The treaty, however, won Senate approval after a long and difficult debate. One result of the conflict over the treaty was the emergence of the two-party system. Jefferson believed that despite the early warnings from George Washington against political parties, the country

WHISKEY REBELLION

Jefferson wanted taxes kept low, and he was among those upset by the levies placed on whiskey by Hamilton's taxing program. In 1794, a small band of whiskey distillers in western Pennsylvania resisted the law and refused to pay the tax. Hamilton wanted to teach them a lesson and convinced President Washington that a show of force was necessary. After the militant farmers burned the home of a local tax collector, Washington ordered an army to the region. Several dozen prisoners were sent to Philadelphia for trial. None were found guilty.

was becoming divided into two camps—Republicans like Jefferson and "monocrats" willing to do Hamilton's bidding on the Federalist side.

Jefferson also saw the harsh measures used to put down the Whiskey Rebellion as an unnecessary show of federal power against tax-oppressed western farmers. By letters and through friends in Congress, Jefferson encouraged the development of an opposition to the Federalist program.

VICE PRESIDENT. As a result of the anti-Hamilton campaign, Jefferson received enough electoral votes in the presidential election of 1796 to become vice president in the administration of John Adams. Jefferson saw Adams as Hamilton's tool. As Federalist legislation continued to raise taxes and restrict free speech, Jefferson was dismayed by Hamilton's continuing influence on national policy. Passage of the Alien and Sedition Acts in 1798 drew Jefferson's anger. Federalists had pushed them through Congress as anti-French measures meant to annoy the Republican opposition. Jefferson secretly wrote the Kentucky Resolutions and encouraged Madison to write the Virginia Resolutions, advancing the concept of states' rights as a protest against the "unconstitutional" Alien and Sedition Acts. The Federalists justified the increased taxes as necessary to

enlarge the pitifully small army and almost non-existent navy.

ELECTION OF 1800. Jefferson insisted that the national debt was actually larger than the Federalists claimed. He and Aaron Burr became active in campaigns to elect Republicans who would dismantle the Federalist program. In the presidential election of 1800, Jefferson easily defeated Adams but was tied with Burr in the Electoral College. Burr had agreed to a Republican plan that would have made Jefferson president by common consent, but Burr went back on his earlier promises. Because of the tie in the Electoral College, the election went to the House of Representatives where Burr was not defeated until the thirty-sixth ballot which came on 17 February 1801. Thereafter, Jefferson had no use for Burr, who became vice president under the Constitution. (The Constitution was later amended to require separate votes in the Electoral College for president and vice president.)

Once he was president, Jefferson found Congress willing to pass his program: lower taxes, drastic cuts in the naval budget, and creation of a military academy at West Point in New York. Jefferson made Madison his secretary of state, and Albert Gallatin became secretary of the treasury. The war in Europe between France and Great Britain spread into a worldwide conflict after 1803, and U.S. ships continued to be stopped by both the French and the British navies. Their attacks forced Jefferson and Madison to work hard to make France and Great Britain acknowledge the right of U.S. ships to sail on the world seas without intimidation.

THE LOUISIANA PURCHASE. The war in Europe created an opportunity for the United States to expand west when Napoleon, the French emperor, seized on a U.S. inquiry about the purchase of New Orleans and instead offered the entire Louisiana Territory to the U.S. envoys for $15 million. Thus the nation acquired some 828,000 square miles of land from the financially hard-pressed French ruler for the bargain price of

FIRST INAUGURAL ADDRESS

. . . During the contest of opinion through which we have passed the animation of discussions and of exertions has sometimes worn an aspect which might impose on strangers unused to think freely and to speak and to write what they think; but this being now decided by the voice of the nation, announced according to the rules of the Constitution, all will, of course, arrange themselves under the will of the law, and unite in common efforts for the common good. All, too, will bear in mind this sacred principle, that though the will of the majority is in all cases to prevail, that will to be rightful must be reasonable; that the minority possess their equal rights, which equal law must protect, and to violate would be oppression. Let us, then, fellow-citizens, unite with one heart and one mind. Let us restore to social intercourse that harmony and affection without which liberty and even life itself are but dreary things. And let us reflect that, having banished from our land that religious intolerance under which mankind so long bled and suffered, we have yet gained little if we countenance a political intolerance as despotic, as wicked, and capable of as bitter and bloody persecutions. During the throes and convulsions of the ancient world, during the agonizing spasms of infuriated man, seeking through blood and slaughter his long-lost liberty, it was not wonderful that the agitation of the billows should reach even this distant and peaceful shore; that this should be more felt and feared by some and less by others, and should divide opinions as to measures of safety. But every difference of opinion is not a difference of principle. We have called by different names brethren of the same principle. We are all Republicans, we are all Federalists. If there be any among us who would wish to dissolve this Union or to change its republican form, let them stand undisturbed as monuments of the safety with which error of opinion may be tolerated where reason is left free to combat it. I know, indeed, that some honest men fear that a republican government can not be strong, that this Government is not strong enough; but would the honest patriot, in the full tide of successful experiment, abandon a government which has so far kept us free and firm on the theoretic and visionary fear that this Government, the world's best hope, may by possibility want energy to presence itself? I trust not. I believe this, on the contrary, the strongest Government on earth. I believe it the only one where every man, at the call of the law, would fly to the standard of the law, and would meet invasions of the public order as his own personal concern. Sometimes it is said that man can not be trusted with the government of himself. Can he, then, be trusted with the government of others? Or have we found angels in the forms of kings to govern him? Let history answer this question. . . .

About to enter, fellow-citizens, on the exercise of duties which comprehend everything dear and valuable to you, it is proper you should understand what I deem the essential principles of our Government, and consequently those which ought to shape its Administration. I will compress them within the narrowest compass they will bear, stating the general principle, but not all its limitations. Equal and exact justice to all men, of whatever state or persuasion, religious or political; peace, commerce, and honest friendship with all nations, entangling alliances with none; the support of the State governments in all their rights, as the most competent administrations for our domestic concerns and the surest bulwarks against antirepublican tendencies; the preservation of the General Government in its whole constitutional vigor, as the sheet anchor of our peace at home and safety abroad; a jealous care of the right of election by the people—a mild and safe corrective of abuses which are lopped by the sword of revolution where peaceable remedies are unprovided; absolute acquiescence in the decisions of the majority, the vital principle of republics, from which is no appeal but to force, the vital principle and immediate parent of despotism; a well-disciplined militia, our best reliance in peace and for the first moments of war, till regulars may relieve them; the supremacy of the civil over the military authority; economy in the public expense, that labor may be lightly burthened; the honest payment of our debts and sacred preservation of the public faith; encouragement of agriculture, and of commerce as its handmaid; the diffusion of information and arraignment of all abuses at the bar of the public reason; freedom of religion; freedom of the press, and freedom of person under the protection of the habeas corpus, and trial by juries impartially selected. these principles form the bright constellation which has gone before us and guided our steps through an age of revolution and reformation. The wisdom of our sages and blood of our heroes have been devoted to their attainment. They should be the creed of our political faith, the text of civic instruction, the touchstone by which to try the services of those we trust; and should we wander from them in moments of error or of alarm, let us hasten to retrace our steps and to regain the road which alone leads to peace, liberty, and safety.

I repair, then, fellow-citizens, to the post you have assigned me. With experience enough in subordinate offices to have seen the difficulties of this the greatest of all, I have learnt to expect that it will rarely fall to the lot of imperfect man to retire from this station with the reputation and the favor which bring him into it. Without pretensions to that high confidence you reposed in our first and greatest revolutionary character, whose preeminent services had entitled him to the first place in his country's love and destined for him the fairest page in the volume of faithful history, I ask so much confidence only as may give firmness and effect to the legal administration of your affairs. I shall often go wrong through defect of judgment. When right, I shall often be thought wrong by those whose positions will not command a view of the whole ground. I ask your indulgence for my own errors, which will never be intentional, and your support against the errors of others, who may condemn what they would not if seen in all its parts. The approbation implied by your suffrage is a great consolation to me for the past, and my future solicitude will be to retain the good opinion of those who have bestowed it in advance, to conciliate that of others by doing them all the good in my power, and to be instrumental to the happiness and freedom of all. . . .

• *Thomas Jefferson's inauguration marked the first time in U.S. history that power passed from one political party to another. To Jefferson, the people were the ultimate source of a government's authority. As a political philosopher, he had an abiding faith in democracy. While he preached democracy, he was also a slaveholding country gentleman with a classical education and exquisite tastes. Perhaps Jefferson represented the conscience of the United States—and the true core values of the American revolution.*

According to a popular myth, Thomas Jefferson, unattended by a living soul, rode up the Capitol hill, tied his horse to the picket fence, entered the Senate chamber, and took the presidential oath exactly at noon, 4 March 1801. Although this story is not true, it served for many generations to illustrate the inauguration of the "Man of the People." In reality, Jefferson, surrounded by a crowd, left his boardinghouse and walked to the unfinished Capitol building—the first president to take the oath in the new city of Washington. The ceremony was held in the small Senate chamber. Afterward, the President read his inaugural address in such a low voice that he almost could not be heard.

The Louisiana Purchase doubled the size of the United States for the bargain price of 3.5 cents an acre. (Drawing by Vincent Robert Evans.)

"Fearing that France might close the port of New Orleans and thus affect the commerce of the inland United States, Jefferson sent James Monroe as a special envoy to Paris to join with Robert Livingston, minister to France, in an effort to purchase an area at the mouth of the Mississippi that would forever protect the freedom of American shipping. Instead of offerring New Orleans and East and West Florida for sale, Napoleon's foreign minister, Charles Maurice de Talleyrand, jarred Livingston—and eventually the American government—by offering to sell the entire territory. The effect on American growth was to be monumental, and an immediate result was the transformation of the Lewis and Clark Expedition from a low-profile, 'literary' examination of another country's terrain to a public undertaking that a whole nation could watch and support."

• *Donald Jackson, "The West,"* Thomas Jefferson, A Reference Biography, *edited by Merrill D. Peterson.*

3.5 cents an acre. Even Federalists knew a bargain when they saw one; the Louisiana Purchase was ratified by the U.S. Senate on 20 October 1803 and the territory was transferred to the United States on 20 December 1803. Never before had one nation taken such a huge piece of territory from another nation without a war. The purchase doubled the size of the United States. It was perfect timing, just before an election year.

FREEDOM OF RELIGION. Jefferson went out of his way to pledge that the federal government would not interfere in citizens' liberties, and pledged to keep "a wall of separation" between church and state. Scorned by much of the New England clergy for his religious beliefs, Jefferson took pains to make those beliefs clear. He had hardly been inaugurated when he wrote: "The Christian religion, when divested of the rags in

LETTER TO ROBERT R. LIVINGSTON
18 APRIL 1802

. . . The cession of Louisiana and the Floridas by Spain to France, works most sorely on the United States. On this subject the Secretary of State has written to you fully, yet I cannot forbear recurring to it personally, so deep is the impression it makes on my mind. It completely reverses all the political relations of the United States, and will form a new epoch in our political course. Of all nations of any consideration, France is the one which, hitherto, has offered the fewest points on which we could have any conflict of right, and the most points of a communion of interests. From these causes, we have ever looked to her as our natural friend, as one with which we could never have an occasion of difference. Her growth, therefore, we viewed as our own, her misfortunes ours. There is on the globe one single spot, the possessor of which is our natural and habitual enemy. It is New Orleans, through which the produce of three-eighths of our territory must pass to market, and from its fertility it will ere long yield more than half of our whole produce and contain more than half of our inhabitants. France, placing herself in that door, assumes to us the attitude of defiance. Spain might have retained it quietly for years. Her pacific dispositions, her feeble state, would induce her to increase our facilities there so that her possession of the place would hardly be felt by us, and it would not, perhaps, be very long before some circumstance might arise, which might make the cession of it to us the price of something of more worth to her. Not so can it ever be in the hands of France: the impetuosity of her temper, the energy and restlessness of her character, placed in a point of eternal friction with us, and our character, which, though quiet and loving peace and the pursuit of wealth, is high-minded, despising wealth in competition with insult or injury, enterprising and energetic as any nation on earth; these circumstances render it impossible that France and the United States can continue long friends, when they meet in so irritable a position. They, as well as we, must be blind if they do not see this; and we must be very improvident if we do not begin to make arrangements on that hypothesis. The day that France takes possession of New Orleans, fixes the sentence which is to restrain her forever within her low-water mark. It seals the union of two nations, who, in conjunction, can maintain exclusive possession of the ocean. From that moment, we must marry ourselves to the British fleet and nation. We must turn all our attention to a maritime force, for which our resources place us on very high ground; and having formed and connected together a power which may render reinforcement of her settlements here impossible to France, make the first cannon which shall be fired in Europe the signal for the tearing up of any settlement she may have made, and for holding the two continents of America in sequestration for the common purposes of the United British and American nations. This is not a state of things we seek or desire. . . .

• *Spain had obtained the vast Louisiana Territory from France in 1762. But in 1800, Spain ceded the area back to France. Jefferson became concerned that a new French empire in North America could threaten U.S. commerce. He instructed Robert R. Livingston, U.S. minister to France, to persuade the Emperor Napoleon to sell the city of New Orleans, an indispensable port for western farmers. Napoleon, recently defeated in Saint-Domingue (later called Haiti), the most valuable of the French colonies in the Americas—and in need of money to finance his European wars—offered to sell the entire Louisiana Territory to the United States. On 20 December 1803, the United States formally took possession.*

In this letter to Livingston, Jefferson expressed his thoughts on the importance of New Orleans to the United States.

This portrait of Thomas Jefferson was painted by Rembrandt Peale in Philadelphia, Pennsylvania in 1805. It shows Jefferson nearing his sixty-second birthday and shortly before his second inauguration as president. (Courtesy National Archives.)

which they have enveloped it, and brought to the original purity and simplicity of its benevolent institutor, is a religion of all others most friendly to liberty, science, and the freest expansion of the human mind." His critics were not silenced, but Jefferson's repeated warnings that churches and religious beliefs must never be interfered with by the government, at any level, became the hallmark of his republicanism.

ELECTION OF 1804. For the 1804 election, Aaron Burr was dropped from the ticket. Indeed, at the Democratic-Republican nominating caucus, Burr was not even considered for renomination to the vice presidency. Instead, George Clinton of New York was chosen as Jefferson's running mate.

The Federalist presidential candidate was Charles C. Pinckney, but he had little chance of defeating the popular president. Jefferson received 162 electoral votes to Pinckney's 14.

Congress was so agreeable that in Jefferson's eight years as president, Jefferson never vetoed a single law. This record, never repeated by any president, testifies to the harmony between the president and Congress. Federalists were such a minority that they were powerless to stop Jefferson's dismantling of the programs they had enacted between 1789 and 1800.

IMPRESSMENT. There were some failures during Jefferson's administration. He was frustrated by the repeated harassment of U.S. shipping by the French

JEFFERSON TO CONGRESS
18 DECEMBER 1807

The communications now made, showing the great and increasing dangers with which our vessels, our seamen, and merchandise are threatened on the high seas and elsewhere from the belligerent powers of Europe, and it being of the greatest importance to keep in safety these essential resources, I deem it my duty to recommend the subject to the consideration of Congress, who will doubtless perceive all the advantages which may be expected from an inhibition of the department of our vessels from the ports of the United States.

Their wisdom will also see the necessity of making every preparation for whatever events may grow out of the present crisis.

• *Between 1789 and 1815, four presidents had to deal with revolutionary events sweeping across Europe—and the problem of keeping the United States out of the conflicts while, at the same time, profiting through trade with the warring nations. Eventually, the United States became involved in a second war with Great Britain (War of 1812 [1812–1815]).*

The wars in Europe caught the United States in the middle—the British navy blockaded Napoleon's empire, and he retaliated with decrees prohibiting neutral nations, such as the United States, from trading with Great Britain. Each combatant determined to use power to prevent its opponent from benefiting from U.S. trade. Diplomatic attempts to ease these commercial restrictions failed. Finally, President Jefferson decided to use U.S. economic pressure to stop both Great Britain and France from interfering with U.S. shipping. He thought that by halting trade with both nations, they each would suffer economically, and they would cease obstructing U.S. commerce.

On 18 December 1807, Jefferson asked Congress for "an inhibition of the departure of our vessels from the ports of the United States." The Embargo Act (1807), however, had the reverse effect. (An embargo is an economic boycott, that ends trade with another nation.) The value of U.S. exports fell from $108 million in 1807 to $22 million in 1808. Businesses failed. Shipbuilding stopped. Wheat plunged from $2 a bushel to 75¢. Tobacco filled the idle waterfronts. Jefferson's critics accused him of ruining the country. Three days before the end of his term, on 1 March 1809, Jefferson signed a congressional resolution repealing the Embargo Act.

and the British navies. Twisting international law to fit its own circumstances, each country made it illegal for U.S. merchants to trade with its enemy and seized U.S. seamen and cargoes in alarming numbers. By 1806, the British navy intensified its campaign to bring U.S. commerce on the high seas to a standstill and, hard-pressed for crews, stepped up the practice of stopping U.S. ships and seizing sailors who were said to be deserters, a practice known as impressment. Hundreds of U.S. seamen were pressed into service, a few were executed, and many imprisoned in British jails.

Jefferson sent envoys to London to negotiate an end to these practices. One of the U.S. diplomats, Jefferson's friend James Monroe, thought he had solved some of the problems and signed a treaty with the British. Because the issue of impressment was left unresolved, Jefferson never submitted the treaty to the Senate for ratification. Jefferson seems to have considered declaring war on both Great Britain and France, mainly as a legal device to force the issue of seizures at sea, but he was not eager to rush into a shooting war. A war almost broke out, however, when the British ship *Leopard* waited off the Virginia coast and fired on the U.S. ship *Chesapeake*. The nation reacted with fury, but Jefferson avoided a war by allowing time for the country's war fever to cool.

THE BURR CONSPIRACY. Jefferson had been aroused by rumors that his old enemy Aaron Burr had been scheming with some filibusterers, adventurers involved in illegal foreign expeditions, who had a small naval force on the Ohio River. According to reports, Burr planned to use a rag-tag army to found a western republic separate from the United States. Intrigue with a foreign power was strongly suspected. Jefferson had Burr arrested and eventually tried for treason, but a Richmond court refused to convict Burr. In his hatred for Burr, Jefferson showed an unusual streak of malice. Burr's release was one of Jefferson's few disappointments in domestic affairs during his presidency.

The hostility of France and Great Britain toward U.S. shipping was another failure. Jefferson, Madison, and other Republican leaders believed that French and British attacks on U.S. ships displayed a contempt for the United States as a newcomer in the family of nations. Desperate for a solution, Jefferson finally approved a drastic law in 1807 that established a total shutdown of U.S. shipping to foreign ports. The purpose of the Embargo Act was to keep U.S. ships and sailors out of harm's way, but the result was an economic depression in U.S. seaports and a drop in the prices of U.S. farm products on the world market. New England shippers reacted with rage, but loyal Republican farmers withheld their criticism as they tightened their belts. Feeling pressure from businessmen who claimed they faced ruin, Congress repealed the Embargo Act and, in an indirect slap at Jefferson, set its expiration for 4 March 1809, the day Jefferson's second term ended.

Worn out by the arguing in his party and upset by growing signs of opposition in Congress, a weary Jefferson took a back seat during his last year in the White House. Hamilton was killed in a duel with Burr, and the Federalists had no strong person who could replace their fallen leader. Jefferson apparently thought that with James Madison nominated and then elected as his successor, his Republican programs would continue to guide the nation.

REPUBLICAN SIMPLICITY. While in the White House, Jefferson had applied his ideas on republican simplicity to the social calendar. His daughter, Martha Jefferson Randolph, had sometimes been his official hostess and other times Dolley Madison had been helpful. Jefferson never entertained lavishly and was in fact criticized by foreign diplomats for his lack of style. One minister even resented the fact that when he was first presented to Jefferson as an official envoy, the President met him while wearing his house slippers. Jefferson may have tried to avoid lavish entertainment because he needed his $25,000 annual salary to help pay his debts, but for whatever reason, he did not like the parties that he believed violated his code of republican simplicity.

RETIREMENT. Back at his beloved Monticello, Jefferson kept alive his interest in national policy. He supported the war with Great Britain that began in 1812 and thought that "man for man, and gun for gun," Americans could make the British acknowledge the rights of the United States on the seas and elsewhere. Embittered Federalists raised the cry in 1813 that Jefferson was now critical of Washington, but Jefferson quickly countered that he and Washington had always been in agreement on basic principles: "The only point on which he and I ever differed in opinion, was, that I had more confidence than he had in the natural integrity and discretion of the people, and in the safety and extent to which they might trust themselves with a control over their government."

Jefferson proposed a drastic overhaul of Virginia's education system. He favored a system

LETTER TO ROGER C. WEIGHTMAN
MONTICELLO, 24 JUNE 1826

Respected Sir,—The kind invitation I receive from you, on the part of the citizens of the city of Washington, to be present with them at their celebration on the fiftieth anniversary of American Independence, as one of the surviving signers of an instrument pregnant with our own, and the fate of the world, is most flattering to myself, and heightened by the honorable accompaniment proposed for the comfort of such a journey. It adds sensibly to the sufferings of sickness, to be deprived by it of a personal participation in the rejoicings of that day. But acquiescence is a duty, under circumstances not placed among those we are permitted to control. I should, indeed, with peculiar delight, have met and exchanged there congratulations personally with the small band, the remnant of that host of worthies, who joined with us on that day, in the bold and doubtful election, we were to make for our country, between submission or the sword; and to have enjoyed with them the consolatory fact, that our fellow citizens, after half a century of experience and prosperity, continue to approve the choice we made. May it be to the world, what I believe it will be, (to some parts sooner, to others later, but finally to all,) the signal of arousing men to burst the chains under which monkish ignorance and superstition had persuaded them to bind themselves, and to assume the blessings and security of self-government. That form which we have substituted, restores the free right to the unbounded exercise of reason and freedom of opinion. All eyes are opened, or opening, to the rights of man. The general spread of the light of science has already laid open to every view the palpable truth, that the mass of mankind has not been born with saddles on their backs, nor a favored few booted and spurred, ready to ride them legitimately, by the grace of God. These are grounds of hope for others. For ourselves, let the annual return of this day forever refresh our recollections of these rights, and an undiminished devotion to them.

I will ask permission here to express the pleasure with which I should have met my ancient neighbors of the city of Washington and its vicinities, with whom I passed so many years of a pleasing social intercourse; an intercourse which so much relieved the anxieties of the public cares, and left impressions so deeply engraved in my affections, as never to be forgotten. With my regret that illhealth forbids me the gratification of an acceptance, be pleased to receive for yourself, and those for whom you write, the assurance of my highest respect and friendly attachments.

• *Thomas Jefferson's reply to the chairman of a proposed Independence Day celebration in Washington was written less than two weeks before his death. It is Jefferson's last existing letter.*

---

that would emphasize natural talent in students and reward those who showed a combination of hard work and cleverness. At the center of his system was a state university. Jefferson was instrumental in the final decision to place Virginia's state university only a few miles from Monticello. Chartered in 1819, the University of Virginia was built on an architectural plan designed by Jefferson. It opened for instruction in 1825, with Jefferson as its first rector.

FINANCIAL WOES. Financial ruin faced Jefferson in his last years. Already under a heavy debt load, Jefferson was near bankruptcy after 1819, when he was saddled with an additional $20,000 loss by a careless friend whose note Jefferson had endorsed. He tried without success to sell some land. However, land was greatly depreciated by the panic of 1819, the nation's first major depression, which sank farm and land prices to unreasonable lows. In desperation, Jefferson tried to hold a public lottery to dispose of Monticello, but news of this situation brought a national response and some contributions. The lottery was called off, but Jefferson's estate was still a shambles at his death on 4 July 1826.

Jefferson's death came as the nation celebrated the 50th year of national independence. He had been invited to a ceremony planned in Washington, but ill health (among other reasons) forced him to decline. He sent a message for the ceremony, however, that summed up Jefferson's ideas on human freedom. Because of the events of 4 July 1776, he noted, "All eyes are opened, or opening, to the rights of man. The general spread of the light of science has already laid open to every view the palpable [obvious] truth, that the mass of mankind has not been born with saddles on their backs, nor a favored few booted and spurred, ready to ride them legitimately, by the grace of God. These are grounds of hope for others."

He was buried at the family cemetery at Monticello. He had designed his own tombstone and written the inscription it bears:

Here was buried
Thomas Jefferson
Author of the Declaration of American
Independence
of the statute of Virginia for religious freedom
& Father of the University of Virginia

The head of Thomas Jefferson (second from left) is carved on a granite cliff in the Black Hills of South Dakota. The place is Mount Rushmore National Monument and its sculptor, Gutzon Borglum, conceived it as a shrine to American democracy. It includes George Washington (left), Abraham Lincoln (right), and Theodore Roosevelt (second from right).

President Calvin Coolidge dedicated the memorial in 1927 and President Franklin D. Roosevelt dedicated the Jefferson section in 1936. (Courtesy National Archives.)

VICE PRESIDENT

Aaron Burr
(1756-1836)

CHRONOLOGICAL EVENTS

1756	Born, Newark, New Jersey, 6 February
1772	Graduated from College of New Jersey (now Princeton)
1775	Served in the Continental army
1784	Elected to New York State Assembly
1789	Elected attorney general of New York
1791	Elected to U.S. Senate
1800	Elected vice president
1804	Killed Alexander Hamilton in duel at Weehawken, New Jersey, 11 July
1807	Acquitted of charges of treason
1836	Died, Port Richmond, Staten Island, New York, 14 September

BIOGRAPHY

The grandson of the great preacher Jonathan Edwards, Aaron Burr prepared for the ministry until he switched to more worldly pursuits. He studied law and volunteered to fight in the American Revolution. Distinguished in battle, Burr rose to be a colonel in command of his own regiment.

Moving to New York, Burr entered politics as an anti-Federalist in opposition to the Federalists, led by Alexander Hamilton. In 1791, Burr defeated Hamilton's father-in-law for a seat in the U.S. Senate. As senator, Burr opposed Treasury Secretary Hamilton's financial programs. In 1796, Republicans chose Burr to run for vice president with Thomas Jefferson. John Adams won the election, and Jefferson, having received the second largest number of electoral votes, became vice president. In 1800, Jefferson and Burr ran again and defeated the Federalists, but both men received the same number of electoral votes. The election went to the U.S. House of Representatives, where Federalists tried to block Jefferson by supporting Burr, who did not object.

After 36 ballots, Hamilton finally persuaded the Federalists that Jefferson represented the lesser of the two evils and Jefferson was elected president. As Jefferson's vice president, Burr never regained the President's confidence. He presided over the Senate with dignity and skill, but Senate Republicans saw him as an opportunist.

In February 1804, the Republican Caucus chose New York Governor George Clinton to replace Burr as the Republican candidate for vice president. Burr responded by campaigning to succeed Clinton as governor. He lost a bitter election and blamed his defeat on his perpetual rival Hamilton, whom he challenged to a duel. At Weehawken, New Jersey, on 11 July 1804, Burr shot and fatally wounded Hamilton.

Fleeing from indictment for murder, Burr then traveled to the West. He schemed to persuade the Western states to leave the Union and form a confederacy under his leadership. Betrayed by one of his co-conspirators, Burr was arrested and tried on charges of treason. The jury found the evidence insufficient to convict him. Burr lived in Europe until 1812, when he returned to New York. He spent his later years petitioning for a pension for his Revolutionary War military service.

VICE PRESIDENT

George Clinton
(1739–1812)

CHRONOLOGICAL EVENTS

1739	Born, Little Britain, New York, 26 July
1759	Appointed clerk of common pleas for Ulster County
1765	Appointed district attorney
1768	Elected to New York State Assembly
1775	Elected to Second Continental Congress
1777	Served as brigadier general in the Continental army
1777	Elected governor of New York
1804	Elected vice president with Thomas Jefferson
1808	Elected vice president with James Madison
1812	Died, Washington, D.C., 20 April

BIOGRAPHY

A Revolutionary War hero, George Clinton was the son of Irish immigrants who settled in upstate New York. Learning surveying from his father, Clinton grew wealthy through land speculation. A large, powerfully-built man, Clinton also had a commanding presence that gained him respect in war and politics.

At age 18, he fought in the French and Indian War. After the war, he studied law, opened a law practice in New York, and became district attorney. Adopting anti-British politics, Clinton served in the New York State Assembly and in the Second Continental Congress. A man of action rather than of speeches, Clinton resigned from Congress to become a brigadier general in the New York militia. He commanded troops that prevented the relief of the British forces at Saratoga, causing a British surrender that was a major turning point in the war.

Elected governor of New York, Clinton at first supported the call for a stronger central government. Over time, however, he grew fearful that the federal government might overwhelm the states by competing for revenues from taxes and tariffs. As the presiding officer at the New York ratifying convention, Clinton opposed the new Constitution. Once the Constitution was adopted, Clinton's supporters promoted him for vice president, but he received only three electoral votes.

Exhausted and in declining health, Clinton retired as governor in 1795. Then in 1801 he left retirement to win another term as governor. Clinton ran largely to keep Vice President Aaron Burr—a man he distrusted—from dominating New York State politics. Clinton's political standing rose and fell depending upon Burr's fate. Also suspicious of Burr, President Thomas Jefferson turned to Clinton for advice for patronage appointments in New York. When the Republican Caucus dropped Burr as a candidate for vice president in 1804, it nominated Governor Clinton to replace him. This switch enabled Republicans to hold New York's large electoral vote. But once the threat from Burr was gone, Jefferson no longer consulted Clinton about patronage.

Despite his age, poor health, and lack of influence in the administration, Clinton hoped to succeed Jefferson as president. Instead, Republicans again nominated him for vice president, in 1808, on a ticket headed by James Madison.

THE CABINET

SECRETARY OF STATE
James Madison, 1801

SECRETARY OF WAR
Henry Dearborn, 1801

SECRETARY OF THE TREASURY
Samuel Dexter, 1801
Albert Gallatin, 1801, 1805

POSTMASTER GENERAL
Joseph Habersham, 1801
Gideon Granger, 1801, 1805

ATTORNEY GENERAL
Levi Lincoln, 1801
John Breckinridge, 1805
Caesar A. Rodney, 1807

SECRETARY OF THE NAVY
Benjamin Stoddert, 1801
Robert Smith, 1801

(Courtesy Library of Congress.)

Albert Gallatin (1761–1849). Gallatin was born in Geneva, Switzerland and emigrated to the United States at age 19. From 1795 to 1801, he served as a congressman from Pennsylvania and became the leader of the Republican minority in the House of Representatives. His superb grasp of finance and his criticism of Federalist financial policies led to the formation of a House committee on finance. Gallatin served on this committee until 1801, when he was appointed secretary of the treasury by President Thomas Jefferson. He was reappointed by President James Madison in 1809.

As secretary of the treasury, under both Jefferson and Madison, Gallatin dramatically reduced the federal debt. His programs of financial reform and economy were virtually destroyed by the War of 1812.

In 1814, Gallatin was a member of the peace commission that negotiated the Treaty of Ghent, ending the War of 1812. He served as U.S. minister to France from 1816 to 1823 and U.S. minister to Great Britain from 1826 to 1827.

Gallatin is called the "Father of American Ethnology." He wrote "A Synopsis of the Indian Tribes . . . of North America" (1836) and founded the American Ethnology Society (1842). In his pioneer work, Gallatin classified North American Indians by linguistic families.

FAMILY

CHRONOLOGICAL EVENTS

30 October 1748	Martha Wayles born	27 September 1772	Daughter, Martha (Patsy), born
20 November 1766	Martha Wayles married Bathurst Skelton	1 August 1778	Daughter, Mary (Polly), born
30 September 1768	Bathurst Skelton died	6 September 1782	Martha Jefferson died
1 January 1772	Martha Wayles Skelton married Thomas Jefferson	17 April 1804	Polly died
		4 July 1826	Thomas Jefferson died

(Courtesy Library of Congress.)

Martha Wayles Skelton was a 23-year-old widow when she married Thomas Jefferson. She died 10 years later, probably weakened by seven pregnancies.

They had two daughters who lived to maturity: Martha (Patsy) and Mary (Polly). Polly died at age 25 after giving birth to her second child. Patsy (pictured here) lived in Paris with her father, and they were devoted to each other. In 1790, she married Thomas Mann Randolph who later became governor of Virginia. She served as official hostess for a time when her father was president. She had 12 children who lived to adulthood, and she named them after famous Americans. Her son, James Madison, was the first child born in the White House. Born later were Benjamin Franklin, Meriweather Lewis, and George Wythe.

My Dear Patsy:

I received yesterday at Marseilles your letter of March 25th; and I received it with pleasure, because it announced to me that you were well. . . . I have received letters which inform me that our dear Polly will certainly come to us this summer. . . When she arrives, she will become a precious charge on your hands. The difference of your age and your common loss of a mother, will put that office on you. Teach her to be always true; no vice is so mean as the want of truth, and at the same time so useless. Teach her never to be angry: anger only serves to torment ourselves, to divert others, and alienate their esteem. . . . If ever you find yourself in difficulty, and doubt how to extricate yourself, do what is right, and you will find it the easiest way of getting out of the difficulty. Do it for the additional incitement of increasing the happiness of him who loves you infinitely. . . .

The Life and Selected Writings of Thomas Jefferson, edited by Adrienne Koch and William Peden.

• Thomas Jefferson wrote this letter to his daughter on 7 April 1787, when she was 15 years old. He wrote often to both daughters, always offering fatherly advice.

MONTICELLO

P.O. Box 217 • Charlottesville, Virginia 22902 • Tel: (804) 295-8181

Thomas Jefferson sketched the original plans for Monticello in 1767. For the next four decades, he was constantly involved with the construction and enlargement of the mansion and grounds.
(Photograph by A. A. M. van der Heyden.)

Located on Route 53, three miles southeast of Charlottesville. Open daily, March through October, from 8 A.M. to 5 P.M., and November through February from 9 A.M. to 4:30 P.M. Closed Christmas. Admission fee, with discounts available for groups. Guided tours are offered daily from 8 A.M. to 5 P.M. School programs for all grades are available; reservations required. For more information, call: the Monticello Education Department at (804) 984-9853. A visitor center is located approximately two miles west of Monticello, on Route 20 South at Interstate 64. The center contains the "Thomas Jefferson at Monticello" exhibition and a museum shop. Owned and operated by the Thomas Jefferson Memorial Foundation, Inc., a private, nonprofit organization.

The construction of Monticello began in 1769, when Thomas Jefferson was 26 years old. He inherited the land from his father, Peter, who was a successful planter and surveyor. Jefferson named the mansion after the Italian word for "little mountain." The small garden house at the end of the south terrace was the first building erected; it was completed by January 1772. It is referred to as the Honeymoon Cottage because Jefferson and his wife, Martha, lived there when they were first married.

In 1789, after the death of his wife, Jefferson returned home from France and began to double the size of Monticello. As a result of Jefferson's frequent absences, the changes were not completed for 20 years.

There are 33 rooms in the mansion itself, and 10 workrooms in the outer buildings. In 1795, Jefferson installed wood-burning stoves in some rooms, but the mansion still was heated primarily by fireplaces. The grounds include two orchards, ornamental and vegetable gardens, a vineyard, and an 18-acre grove. The Thomas Jefferson Memorial Foundation has funded restoration projects for over 50 years, including the extensive and detailed re-creation of the flower and vegetable gardens and orchards as laid out by Jefferson.

JEFFERSON MEMORIAL

Tidal Basin, south end of Fifteenth Street, SW • Washington, D.C. • Tel: (202) 426-6841

Located along the south bank of the Tidal Basin, in a direct line with the White House. Open daily from 8 A.M. to midnight. Closed Christmas. No admission fee. Handicapped accessible. Special tours available. Gift shop and bookstore. For more information, write: National Park Service, Mall Operations, 900 Ohio Drive, SW 20242. A unit of the National Park System.

▲ *Six hundred cherry trees, a gift from Japan in 1912, border the western edge of the Tidal Basin near the Jefferson Memorial.* (Courtesy Library of Congress.)

The memorial was designed by John Russell Pope. He used a design which Jefferson himself used at both Monticello and the University of Virginia. The cornerstone was laid on 15 November 1938. In 1943, on the 200th anniversary of Jefferson's birth, it was officially dedicated.

Above the entranceway, a sculpture group created by Adolph A. Weinman depicts the committee appointed by the Continental Congress to write the Declaration of Independence. A 19-foot bronze statue of Jefferson, sculpted by Rudolph Evans, stands in the center of the domed interior, surrounded by four inscriptions from Jefferson's writings—including the Declaration of Independence and the Virginia Statute for Religious Freedom.

A Marine Honor Guard stood at the base of Jefferson's statue on 12 April 1943. The original Declaration of Independence was placed there to commemorate the 200th anniversary of Jefferson's birth. This statue was made out of plaster of Paris, and it was not cast in bronze until after the end of World War II. (Courtesy Library of Congress.) ▶

James Madison

4TH PRESIDENT

OF THE UNITED STATES OF AMERICA

CHRONOLOGICAL EVENTS

16 March 1751	Born, Port Conway, Virginia
25 September 1771	Graduated from the College of New Jersey (later Princeton University)
25 April 1776	Elected to Virginia Convention, Williamsburg
7 October 1776	Elected to first Virginia House of Delegates
1778	Appointed to Council of State (Virginia)
14 December 1779	Elected to Second Continental Congress
1784	Again elected to Virginia House of Delegates
1786	Again elected to Second Continental Congress
25 May–	Attended Constitutional Convention; offered Virginia Plan 17 September 1787
17 September 1787	Signed the Constitution
1787–1788	With Alexander Hamilton and John Jay, wrote *The Federalist*
2 February 1789	Elected to U.S. House of Representatives
28 September 1789	Introduced the Bill of Rights in First Congress
1791	Led opposition in Congress to Alexander Hamilton's program for a national bank
1798	Wrote Virginia Resolutions
24 April 1799	Again elected to Virginia House of Delegates
5 March 1801	Appointed secretary of state
1808	Elected president
4 March 1809	Inaugurated president
19 June 1812	Congress declared war on Great Britain
1812	Reelected president
4 March 1813	Inaugurated president
24–25 August 1814	Washington, D.C. burned by British troops
24 December 1814	Treaty of Ghent signed, ending War of 1812
1826	Named rector of University of Virginia
1829	Attended Virginia Constitutional Convention
28 June 1836	Died at Montpelier, Orange County, Virginia

BIOGRAPHY

James Madison was born on a Virginia plantation near the Rappahannock River landing at Port Conway, King George County, on 16 March 1751. He was the first of 12 children born to James Madison, Sr. and Nelly Conway Madison. The family moved to Orange County, Virginia, while he was still an infant. His father built the family home there on a plantation of more than 4,000 acres. The land had belonged to Madison's grandfather, Ambrose, who had originally called the place Mount Pleasant. He later changed the name to Montpelier, a word of French origin meaning "a healthy, pleasant place."

From the time he was 12 until he was 18 he was either in a boys' school or taught by private tutors. In the summer of 1769, he entered the College of New Jersey (later Princeton University). The faculty consisted of three tutors and its president, John Witherspoon, a prominent clergyman who later signed the Declaration of Independence (1776). By encouraging his students to enter public service, Witherspoon influenced an entire generation of national leaders. Madison studied very hard and graduated in two years (1771). He later wrote that the effort had endangered his life. In fact, he suffered from a variety of illnesses, both then and later. Nevertheless, he lived to be 85 in a time when bloodletting (controlled bleeding) and the use of bloodsucking leeches were among doctors' common remedies.

When the quarrels of the colonists with England finally erupted into a full-scale revolution, Madison was in Virginia. Because of his family influence and wealth, he was chosen to represent Orange County in the Virginia Convention of 1776 (6 May–5 July 1776). Held in Williamsburg, the convention established a working, loosely controlled government for the new state of Virginia, as it broke all ties with England. Nearly every prominent Virginian was there: Patrick Henry, George Mason (George Washington's replacement), and 25-year-old Madison. Thomas Jefferson and Richard Henry Lee were away, serving in the Continental Congress. Mason was clearly the cleverest man present, and it was left to him to prepare a constitution and Declaration of Rights for Virginia. Both documents became models for other emerging states, and the Declaration of Rights was the most influential document of its kind adopted in the United States prior to the Federal Bill of Rights in 1791. At the convention, Madison proposed to broaden a section in the Declaration dealing with religion. Mason's clause called for religious "toleration," but Madison

expanded that to "the free exercise of religion." "Toleration" was an old word in religious usage. It suggested that the state might support a Christian church established by the state (as in England), while it would allow other dissenting Christian groups to hold services. Eight of the 13 colonies soon noted the difference and made similar provisions when they broke with England and wrote their own state constitutions or bill of rights.

The Declaration of Independence (4 July 1776) proclaimed the birth of a new nation. When the United States of America came into existence Virginia was the largest of the new states. It also had the most people. "We all look up to Virginia for examples," John Adams noted in those stirring times when almost each day saw new experiments in governing. Even before independence was achieved, Madison had sought ways to make individual rights and liberties the legacy of the American Revolution.

Few of the Founding Fathers were his intellectual equals. In fact, Madison ranks among the great statesman of U.S. history. Slight in stature, shy, unimpressive in personality, and stubborn, he had few close friends. However, his talent for writing and reasoning gained him a place in the councils of the new nation. After service on the Virginia Council of State (1778–1779), he was twice chosen as a delegate to the Continental Congress (1780–1783 and 1787–1789). There he gained attention for his knowledge of international law, treaties, and geography. When the New England states seemed ready to trade away to Spain settlers' rights to use the Mississippi River, Madison attacked the plan. In doing this, he impressed other members of Congress with his ability to speak for the growing population west of the Appalachian mountains.

After the peace treaty with England was signed in 1783, Madison worried about the future of the country. Elected to the state legislature, Madison told Thomas Jefferson that he would support a bill guaranteeing religious freedom in Virginia. However, Patrick Henry was trying to gain approval for financial aid for teachers of the

In 1775, Patrick Henry said his famous words, "Give me liberty, or give me death," in the House of Burgesses, Virginia. The next year, he was with James Madison at the Virginia Convention in Williamsburg. However, as the years went by, Henry became more and more conservative. Henry became critical of his friend Thomas Jefferson, who succeeded him as governor of Virginia, and he disagreed with Madison about the separation of church and state and the ratification of the Constitution. (Courtesy National Archives.)

Christian religion. In 1785, Madison wrote his "Memorial & Remonstrance" attacking state support for any denomination. He outmaneuvered Henry and Jefferson's bill passed and became law in 1786.

There were many problems plaguing the new nation and differences of opinion in almost all of the 13 statehouses. Arguments over accumulated debts, the lack of a national currency, and the payment of taxes brought a series of local protests. In western Massachusetts, farmers protested sales of their property because they owed taxes. Led by Daniel Shays, a veteran of the recent war against England, they resorted to armed demonstrations, including a threat to attack the arsenal in Springfield, Massachusetts. Shays's Rebellion in 1786 was quickly put down, but the incident gave frightened Americans an excuse for strong action. Madison was among those calling for a new national government. Assisted by Alexander Hamilton, Madison proposed a meeting of the representatives of the 13 states, in Philadelphia, in 1787. Their task was to consider a drastic revision of the Articles of Confederation, which was the country's first constitution (1777–1789). General George Washington showed his approval by agreeing to serve as a Virginia delegate to the Philadelphia convention. Rhode Island declined to participate, but the other 12 states sent a total of 55 delegates. The meetings began in May 1787 and continued through that September.

A RAMROD FOR REFORM (1787). Known to history as the Federal Convention (or Constitutional Convention), the meetings began with a debate on Madison's draft of a Virginia Plan that hinted at a newly structured and stronger federal government. Madison had been the guiding influence in preparing this blueprint for a national constitution. Issued by the Virginia delegation, Madison's plan called for a national government with three branches (legislative, judicial, and executive). It also called for a bicameral Congress (that is, with two "houses") which would have powers to tax, raise military forces, conduct war, and regulate commerce. Several

compromises were reached to settle some difficult matters, such as the unresolved issue of slavery and the status of small states in a larger Union. These compromises distressed Madison. However, in the interest of harmony and in order to get results, he decided that the final version deserved his support. He vowed to work for ratification (approval) of this proposed Federal Constitution.

Madison's main disappointment revolved around the powers reserved to the states. From past experience, Madison suspected that state legislatures could not be trusted to serve the good of *all* the people. He therefore proposed that the federal government have the power to set aside any offensive state laws. The delegates rejected Madison's idea. He was so upset that he wrote his friend, Thomas Jefferson, that he feared the Constitution was too imperfect to work. Jefferson reassured Madison the final draft was worth supporting. Jefferson also replied that Madison's plan was both too strong and unmanageable, and Madison's harsh curbing of state powers was a case of a patch too big for the hole. In time, Madison agreed.

The Constitution was signed on 17 September 1787. At least 9 of the 13 states had to approve it in elected conventions before it would become operative. Madison plunged into the task of getting public support for it. He knew well that the opposition, the Antifederalists, was strong in several key states, including Virginia. Quick ratification in Delaware, Pennsylvania, New Jersey, and Georgia got the process off to a good start. However, the opposition formed a strong front during the winter of 1787–1788. So, Madison, working with Alexander Hamilton and John Jay (who later became chief justice of the Supreme Court), wrote a series of letters to newspapers explaining the strengths of the proposed constitution. They used the signature of "Publius" and were published as *The Federalist*. They are still used to teach citizens the meaning of the Constitution and to help us understand how a republican form of government can function for the good of the majority. In two of his most famous essays, Madison showed us *(Federalist 10)* how a large country like the United States could have a republican government without falling into the quarrels that had ruined the smaller ancient republics. Recognizing Americans' resentment of authority, Madison made a plea (*Federalist 51*) for self-control. He pointed out that restraints in society were needed for the general welfare of all. "If men were angels," Madison wrote, "no government would be necessary."

While the ratification process was still being hotly argued, Madison returned to Virginia and led the forces promoting adoption of the Constitution. At first, he opposed adding a bill of rights to the Constitution because he thought that listing basic rights was a dangerous step. He changed his tactics when he arrived at the Richmond Convention. Ratify the Constitution, Madison promised the delegates, and its supporters would see that a bill of rights would be added at the first session of the new Congress. The vote was close, but the Constitution was ratified, 89 votes to 79. Madison's compromise helped bring Virginia into the ranks of the ratifying states and assured the ratification of the new Constitution.

Madison soon learned that the victory in Virginia had its price. Patrick Henry had great power in the state legislature, and he was determined to show it. Defeated on the ratification issue, Henry took revenge by denying Madison a seat in the U.S. Senate. If Henry had not bitterly opposed him, Madison would have won easily. Henry also tried to defeat Madison in the race for a congressional seat by pitting James Monroe against his old friend. However, Madison campaigned vigorously and won a seat in the new U.S. House of Representatives.

THE BILL OF RIGHTS. Once the First Congress was organized in New York (the temporary capital), Madison pushed for amendments to the Constitution dealing with the civil rights of Americans. By the fall of 1789, Madison also was advising President Washington on national matters and promoting passage of the amendments, which were popularly called the Bill of Rights.

FEDERALIST 51

. . . But the great security against a gradual concentration of the several powers in the same department, consists in giving to those who administer each department the necessary constitutional means and personal motives to resist encroachments of the others. The provision for defence must in this, as in all other cases, be made commensurate to the danger of attack. Ambition must be made to counteract ambition. The interest of the man must be connected with the constitutional rights of the place. It may be a reflection on human nature, that such devices should be necessary to control the abuses of government. But what is government itself, but the greatest of all reflections on human nature? If men were angels, no government would be necessary. If angels were to govern men, neither external nor internal controls on government would be necessary. In framing a government which is to be administered by men over men, the great difficulty lies in this: you must first enable the government to control the governed; and in the next place oblige it to control itself. A dependence on the people is, no doubt, the primary control on the government; but experience has taught mankind the necessity of auxiliary precautions. . . .

• *Eighty-five articles in defense of the Constitution were published between October 1787 and May 1788. In 1788, these articles were published in book form as* The Federalist. *They were the joint effort of James Madison, Alexander Hamilton, and John Jay.* Federalist 51 *discussed the structure of government and the importance of checks and balances.*

Starting with freedom of religion, the rights included freedom of the press, the right to assemble and petition, and the right to bear arms. (See Volume Eight for the complete text of the Constitution.) Many of the congressmen were very upset about Madison's plan. They felt that the Virginian had made a campaign pledge and was insisting on the amendments only as a political gesture. However, they underestimated Madison's commitment. He rallied public opinion throughout the country in favor of the amendments. Most of what was said in the Senate was still kept secret although debates in the House were public. He used the newspapers to reach the public.

Madison believed in the power of public opinion. He knew firsthand that elected representatives had to listen when voters registered their feelings. This was probably the first time in the country's history where citizens reacted and let their congressmen know how they felt about an issue. After a slow start, the states ratified 10 of the 12 amendments in 1789. The process took two years.

Congress adopted 12 articles amending the Constitution in September 1789, and submitted them to the states for ratification. Article One, dealing with representation in the U.S. House of Representatives, was rejected. Article Two, prohibiting increases in congressional salaries during an elected term, was also rejected. (It became the Twenty-seventh Amendment in 1992.) Because the first two had been cut, articles Three through Twelve became the first 10 amendments to the Constitution (Bill of Rights) in December 1791.

As far as the average citizen was concerned, the Bill of Rights was a useful addition to the Constitution that already kept the government from trampling on their rights. Jefferson had advised Madison in 1787: "A bill of rights is what the people are entitled to against every government on earth & what no just government should refuse, or rest on inferences." On 10 December 1791, it was

Madison was active in the revision of the Articles of Confederation. He sought to call a constitutional convention where he presented his Virginia Plan. He assured the ratification of the Bill of Rights. He earned the distinction of being known as "Father of the Constitution and the Bill of Rights."

Madison is resting his hand on the Constitution in this engraving after the portrait by Thomas Sully. The original hangs in the Corcoran Gallery of Art, Washington, D.C. (Courtesy Library of Congress.)

Jefferson's duty, as secretary of state, to proclaim the Bill of Rights officially ratified. After the battle over the Bill of Rights, Madison became a leader of the majority party in the U.S. House of Representatives and few pieces of significant legislation were passed without his support.

In the spring of 1794, Madison asked Aaron Burr, a mutual friend, to introduce him to Dolley Payne Todd, a wealthy widow. They were married on 15 September 1794. Attractive and outgoing, she was the perfect complement to her shy and quiet husband.

Madison retired from Congress in 1797 in order to take care of the Montpelier plantation. He was tired of the arguing in Congress that had begun during Washington's first term. Jefferson, as the first secretary of state, had helped solve several foreign crises. However, he had become involved in a bitter argument with Secretary of the Treasury Alexander Hamilton over the very nature of government. Hamilton, leading the Federalist Party, wanted to shape the government in the image of the constitutional monarchy then ruling England. The Federalists favored a strong national bank, a public debt, and a powerful military force. Jefferson and Madison both favored a weak banking system, a drastic reduction of the national debt, and a small military force. Above all, they believed that the Federalists under Hamilton had weakened the personal rights of U.S. citizens. The Federalists had passed laws that curbed the press and had caused the imprisonment of outspoken critics. In New England, one such critic actually died in prison.

LEADER OF THE OPPOSITION. Before all these abuses occurred, Jefferson and Madison had broken with Hamilton and actively opposed his program. Jefferson resigned from Washington's cabinet in 1793 and handed Madison the role of opposition leader to Hamilton. The two Virginians agreed about what had to be done and created a political movement through groups known as Democratic-Republican societies. Their goal was to oppose successfully the Federalist Party that

had been created during the struggle for the ratification of the Constitution. Once the federal government was in operation, the Federalists moved to make Hamilton's plans a reality. Madison was upset that President Washington tended to side with Hamilton and the Federalists in most matters.

Washington and Madison were increasingly at odds on specific issues of both domestic and foreign policies. However, they always avoided open criticism of one another. Madison never broke publicly with Washington, but he was pressured by Jefferson to write a series of newspaper essays as a counterattack to articles that had been written by Hamilton, who used the name "Pacificus." Hamilton charged that the Republicans (also called Democrats, both terms meant as insults) were much too pro-French. Jefferson pleaded with Madison, "For God's sake . . . take up your pen . . . and cut him to peices [sic]." Madison wrote under the name "Helvidius," an ancient Roman leader who resisted a stubborn emperor. He responded with five essays printed in newspapers in the late summer of 1793. He later confessed that the task was "the most grating one I ever experienced." Madison claimed that the Federalists were misusing the executive branch of the government. He also said that they were bypassing Congress on foreign policy matters and violating the Constitution. Compared with Hamilton's pro-British writings, the essays showed how far the two main authors of *The Federalist* had drifted since 1788.

By their actions, Jefferson and Madison were creating a political party that would soon challenge the Federalists in state and national elections. After Jefferson left the State Department, Hamilton dominated Washington's cabinet and U.S. policy at home and abroad. Toward the end of Washington's second term, Hamilton had accomplished many of his original goals. A national bank was created; an army and navy had been built out of the skimpy forces left from Revolutionary days; commercial regulations were in force that favored English merchants and manufacturers. Hamilton's critics, including Madison, claimed that the powerful Secretary of the Treasury was keeping the United States in a colonial status, still owing something to Great Britain. In his *Farewell Address* (1796), Washington warned against entangling alliances between the United States and foreign nations. Jefferson believed that Hamilton was even then making it into a country under the domination of Great Britain.

While John Adams was elected as Washington's successor in 1796, Madison had joined Jefferson in efforts to deny Adams the presidency, and they almost succeeded. In the Electoral College created by the Constitution, Adams, the Federalist candidate, received 71 electoral votes and was elected president. Jefferson, the Republican candidate, received 68 electoral votes and became vice president. Encouraged by this vote, Madison and Jefferson looked ahead to 1800 as a year when their Republican Party (the "Democratic" label would return later) could triumph.

ELECTION OF 1800. The continuing arguments between Adams and Hamilton undermined the strength of the Federalists. The differences between the Federalists and the Republicans were further illustrated by the passage of the Alien and Sedition Acts in 1798. They curbed personal freedom and extended the period of residence needed for citizenship from 5 to 14 years. Madison wrote the Virginia Resolutions that condemned the Acts, and Jefferson secretly drafted similar Kentucky Resolutions. These resolutions denounced the Alien and Sedition Acts as unconstitutional seizures of rights reserved to either the states or all the people. Madison called them "alarming infractions" of the Constitution. The Virginia and Kentucky Resolutions unsuccessfully urged other state legislatures to join in seeking repeal of these repressive laws. However, with help from New York, Pennsylvania, and New Jersey, Madison and Jefferson outmaneuvered the Federalists in the 1800 presidential campaign. Jefferson was elected president in a dramatic contest with Aaron Burr that was finally decided by the U.S. House of Representatives. Jefferson appointed Madison secretary of state, a position soon regarded as the stepping-stone to the presidency. After a brief delay caused by the death of his father, Madison was sworn in.

The Jefferson administration soon began to take apart the Federalist tax and military structure. At the same time, it formed a strong political alliance with the nation's farmers. Meanwhile, merchants, shippers, and bankers called for protection from the warring powers in Europe who were seizing U.S. vessels on the high seas. France dominated the European continent while the British navy controlled the Atlantic and Mediterranean sea lanes. Keeping the country out of a war with either France or England, or both, became Madison's major concern.

In 1803, the United States purchased the vast Louisiana Territory from France. As secretary of state, Madison sent William C.C. Claiborne, governor of Mississippi Territory, to make the formal acceptance of Louisiana from the French. He did so at New Orleans on 20 December 1803. Payments of $15 million secured 828 thousand square miles for the United States. Never before in history had so much land changed hands, from one nation to another, without a shot fired.

Madison believed the biggest problem facing the United States was the seizure of U.S. sailors on the high seas by the British navy. In need of sailors for their ships, the English stopped U.S. vessels to search for British subjects and those they considered to be deserters. Such tactics appeared to make a mockery of American independence. The impudence of the British navy insulted American pride. Madison's report to Congress (20 January 1806) on British infringement of America's neutral rights and the impressment (kidnapping) of American seamen was followed by a U.S. Senate resolution attacking the seizures as "an unprovoked aggression." Great Britain paid no attention to the American protests.

UNDECLARED WAR ON THE OCEANS. When the British ship *Leopard* fired on the U.S. frigate

Chesapeake in 1807, anti-British feelings reached a new high. The *Chesapeake* was severely damaged; 3 crew members were killed and 18 were wounded, including the ship's commander. Neither Jefferson nor Madison wanted another war with Great Britain. Negotiations for British payments to compensate for the lives lost and the damage to the ship proceeded, but American public opinion demanded stronger action. The scholarly Madison searched international agreements to support his position that "free ships make free goods." The idea was that U.S. ships were neutral, and therefore could not be seized as legal contraband by warring powers. Similarly, Madison claimed a sailor on a ship flying the U.S. flag was not subject to British laws or impressment.

Finally, a frustrated Madison and Jefferson decided to keep all U.S. ships in port. They supported a drastic measure, the Embargo Act, a self-imposed boycott of world commerce. This quarantine on trade ruined U.S. shipping and commerce for a while. The Embargo Act divided the nation. Thousands of sailors were thrown out of work and many merchants lost everything. Stores of wheat, cotton, and tobacco piled up on docks. Still, for a time at least, Jefferson found Congress and the people willing to sacrifice to keep the United States from becoming involved in a European war.

In the presidential election of 1808, Jefferson used his influence to have the Republicans nominate James Madison. The Federalists chose Charles Cotesworth Pinckney, a diplomat and soldier from South Carolina who had been Washington's aide-de-camp during the Revolution. As was the rule, presidential candidates were not expected to campaign for the office, but simply went about their business. They did not make speeches nor issue statements. The campaigning was left to party officials, political leaders, and newspaper editors. Madison took the popular vote, winning easily in the Electoral College. He came into the presidency with the nation awaiting some dramatic action that would break the deadlock in international relations.

Congress repealed the Embargo Act in 1809, but this did not resolve the commercial crisis. As the war between Great Britain and France raged on, Great Britain issued orders that tried to stop neutral commerce with France. The Royal Navy tried to enforce the blockade of France's ports and that often involved seizing U.S. cargoes and crews. They occasionally executed those accused of desertion. Napoleon, the French emperor, retaliated by issuing a series of decrees that also prohibited neutral countries from trading with Great Britain. France also seized U.S. ships and imprisoned their crews.

Madison searched for an honorable solution to the American problem. Congress passed a law, known as Macon's Bill No. 2, after the North Carolinian whose name appeared on the legislation. It provided that if either Great Britain or France called off their attacks on U.S. shipping, U.S. ports would become open to them. If one nation agreed, the other would have three months to do the same. If they did not, then all trade with that nation would stop.

Napoleon thought that this law offered him an opportunity to trick both Great Britain and the United States, and perhaps even to provoke a war between the two. He claimed to have issued a letter ending all French attacks on U.S. shipping providing Great Britain did the same. The British claimed that the French were merely playing a diplomatic game, because France continued to capture U.S. cargo and imprison Yankee crews. Madison accepted the French claim at face value. His critics claimed that he had fallen into a diplomatic trap, but he would not admit it. Madison called on Great Britain to follow France's lead, probably hoping that the British would back off. Instead, a diplomatic courier from London arrived in the spring of 1812 with the news that the British cabinet would not change its policy until the French offer turned out to be true. Frustrated and disappointed, Madison sent a war message to Congress in June 1812 rather than accept this latest insult.

REQUEST FOR A DECLARATION OF WAR

. . . British cruisers have been in the continued practice of violating the American flag on the great highway of nations, and of seizing and carrying off persons sailing under it, not in the exercise of a belligerent right founded on the law of nations against an enemy, but of a municipal prerogative over British subjects. . . .

The practice, hence, is so far from affecting British subjects alone that, under the pretext of searching for these, thousands of American citizens, under the safeguard of public law and of their national flag, have been torn from their country and from everything dear to them; have been dragged on board ships of war of a foreign nation and exposed, under the severities of their discipline, to be exiled to the most distant and deadly climes, to risk their lives in the battles of their oppressors, and to be the melancholy instruments of taking away those of their own brethren. . . .

British cruisers have been in the practice also of violating the rights and the peace of our coasts. They hover over and harass our entering and departing commerce. To the most insulting pretensions they have added the most lawless proceedings in our very harbors, and have wantonly spilt American blood within the sanctuary of our territorial jurisdiction. . . .

Not content with these occasional expedients for laying waste our neutral trade, the cabinet of Britain resorted at length to the sweeping system of blockades, under the name of orders in council, which has been molded and managed as might best suit its political views, its commercial jealousies, or the avidity of British cruisers. . . .

It has become, indeed, sufficiently certain that the commerce of the United States is to sacrificed, not as interfering with the belligerent rights of Great Britain; not as supplying the wants of her enemies, which she herself supplies; but as interfering with the monopoly which she covets for her own commerce and navigation. She carries on a war against the lawful commerce of a friend that she may the better carry on a commerce with an enemy—a commerce polluted by the forgeries and perjuries which are for the most part the only passports by which it can succeed. . . .

In reviewing the conduct of Great Britain toward the United States our attention is necessarily drawn to the warfare just renewed by the savages on one of our extensive frontiers—a warfare which is known to spare neither age nor sex and to be distinguished by features peculiarly shocking to humanity. It is difficult to account for the activity and combinations which have for some time been developing themselves among tribes in constant intercourse with British traders and garrisons without connecting their hostility with that influence and without recollecting the authenticated examples of such interpositions heretofore furnished by the officers and agents of that Government. . . .

Whether the United States shall continue passive under these progressive usurpations and these accumulating wrongs, or, opposing force to force in defense of their national rights, shall commit a just cause into the hands of the Almighty Disposer of Events, avoiding all connections which might entangle it in the contest or views of other powers, and preserving a constant readiness to concur in an honorable reestablishment of peace and friendship, is a solemn question which the Constitution wisely confides to the legislative department of the Government. In recommending it to their early deliberations I am happy in the assurance that the decision will be worthy the enlightened and patriotic councils of a virtuous, a free, and a powerful nation. . . .

• *On 1 June 1812, President Madison asked Congress to declare war against Great Britain. Among the reasons he gave were the impressment (kidnapping) of seamen, the blockades, and the warfare conducted by Native Americans who were British allies.*

Oliver Hazard Perry's squadron captured the British naval squadron and won a victory in the Battle of Lake Erie. (Courtesy Library of Congress.)

WAR OF 1812. Congress made blustering threats about the ease with which Canada might be invaded. However, the war went badly once the fighting replaced the boastful speechmaking. Brigadier General William Hull surrendered a force of some 4 thousand Americans to the British at Detroit. The British did not suffer a single casualty. This disgrace overshadowed Madison's conduct of the war from that time on. Inept generals tried to use poorly trained troops, and the New England governors refused to allow their state militias to move beyond their state boundaries. The failure of American leadership often produced confusion among the U.S. troops. The situation on the Great Lakes, however, was different. The heroism of Yankee sailors brought stunning victories. Oliver Hazard Perry went into

action in the Battle of Lake Erie on 10 September 1813 flying a pennant declaring, "Don't Give Up the Ship." When he lost his ship but won the battle, he sent back the message: "We have met the enemy and they are ours." The accomplishments of the small fleet gave American morale the boost it needed. It also strengthened the position of the U.S. peace negotiators.

THE BURNING OF WASHINGTON. Madison's generals, except for Andrew Jackson, were incapable of using their superior forces properly. Nothing symbolized American ineptness as much as the invasion of Washington. On 24 August 1814, outnumbered British troops routed the U.S. forces at Bladensburg, Maryland and marched unopposed into Washington. Once there they set fire to the Capitol, the White House, and many other public buildings. However, the U.S. forces successfully defended Baltimore. The British soon withdrew from the area, and the Madisons returned to Washington where they lived in rented quarters for the rest of his term.

New England Federalists, dissatisfied with the conduct of the war, held a convention at Hartford, Connecticut in December 1814. Disunion was in the air as they drew up demands to be presented to Madison. We now know that some U.S. agents were secretly negotiating with the British in their belief that the war was lost. The British encouraged these New England "negotiators" to think that they might split off from the United States and form a confederation friendly to Great Britain. However, nothing came of this because a ship arrived from Europe with the news that a peace treaty had been signed at Ghent, Belgium, on Christmas Eve, 1814. The Federalists from Hartford had planned to make their demands on 4 February. Instead they went home in near disgrace.

The British fleet attacked Fort McHenry, the major defense of Baltimore, Maryland on 13 September 1814, but they did not capture it or the city. Francis Scott Key, a young Baltimore lawyer, witnessed the bombardment from a ship in the harbor. When he saw that the American flag was still flying the next morning, by dawn's early light, he wrote the words of the "Star-Spangled Banner" on the back of an envelope. The words appeared in a newspaper a week later and it became the national anthem. The battle-scarred flag that flew over Fort McHenry that night is on display in the Smithsonian Institution. (Courtesy Library of Congress.)

THE TREATY OF GHENT. From the moment the War of 1812 began, both sides tried to end the fighting. Representatives of Great Britain and the United States met at Ghent, Belgium in July 1814. Among those sent by the United States were three very able individuals: John Quincy Adams, Henry Clay, and Albert Gallatin. The treaty returned things as they were before the war. It did not contain a word about neutral rights and no land changed hands. The treaty called for no reparations to be paid. It contained a pledge for joint efforts to end the African slave trade. It granted amnesty to the Native American allies of the British-Canadian forces. The two nations agreed to stop fighting and to keep their original boundaries. It did not mention impressment of U.S. sailors because the war in Europe was finally over. The British no longer needed impressment in a world at peace. The U.S. Senate unanimously ratified the Treaty of Ghent on 17 February 1815.

This lithograph by Nathan Currier of Currier and Ives shows the bombardment of Tripoli in 1803. President Thomas Jefferson sent a naval squadron to Tripoli at that time. The piracy continued until 1815 when President James Madison sent a squadron of 10 ships and defeated the pirates. (Courtesy Library of Congress.)

A DIPLOMATIC VICTORY. General Andrew Jackson's forces had almost destroyed a large British army in the Battle of New Orleans on 8 January 1815, two weeks after the peace treaty had been signed. Bonfires and parades across the land celebrated the end of the war. The U.S. negotiators saved the nation's honor, and the peace was seen as an American triumph. Albert Gallatin, who served in the cabinets of both Jefferson and Madison as secretary of the treasury, was one of

Gilbert Stuart painted this portrait of Madison. "In 1817 he left the United States a far stronger nation than it had been in 1809. The new nation was poised for a half-century of expansion, the Constitution was still the polestar of his country's conduct, and he believed that the Union he had done so much to preserve was firmly in place. Madison left Washington and headed for Montpelier a happy man." Robert A. Rutland, "Madison, James: Presidency" in James Madison and the American Nation, 1751–1836, An Encyclopedia.

(Courtesy National Archives.)

the negotiators at Ghent. Upon his return to the United States, he was struck by the general optimism, a widespread feeling that "the war has renewed and reinstated the national feelings and characters which the Revolution had given, and which were daily lessened." "Citizens," Gallatin observed, "are more American; they feel and act more as a nation; and I hope the permanency of the Union is thereby better secured." Twice the United States had taken on the mighty British Empire, and if anything, the War of 1812 solidified the independence gained in the first. After 1814, Americans felt their nation was fit to stand with the leading powers in the world.

Madison was able to benefit from the pride and optimism that surged through the nation during his last years in office. He had long been aware that the national banking system was in bad shape. Madison suggested legislation to Congress that would revive the Bank of the United States to handle the government's business and manage the public debt. Congress passed the legislation. Then Madison began to have doubts. He feared that Congress was violating the Constitution so he vetoed the bill. He then worked with the leaders in both houses, who wrote a measure that he signed into law. He also used his view of the First Amendment as the argument for vetoing a rather harmless bill dealing with some church property. Like Jefferson, Madison wanted to send a strong message supporting a strict interpretation of the Constitution.

Madison tried to keep the country at peace at home but ready to fight on the oceans. He sent a strong naval force under the commands of Stephen Decatur and William Bainbridge to the Barbary coast of North Africa in 1815. The pirates of Morocco, Algiers, Tunis, and Tripoli had been attacking the world's shipping for generations. The squadron of 10 ships under Decatur sailed into Algiers. They were determined to stop the pirates from capturing men and cargoes and holding them for ransom. Annual bribes from most of the western nations, even the United States, had been the pirates'

chief income for decades. Decatur's 44-gun frigate pounded the Algerians until they surrendered. They released all captives and renounced all bribes. Similar treaties were imposed on the other pirates in the area. Only four American lives were lost in these actions and the U.S. Senate ratified the treaty with Algiers in December 1815.

After the Republicans in Congress nominated Secretary of State James Monroe for the presidency, Madison was prepared to hand the office over to him. The opposition Federalist Party had all but disappeared in most sections of the country. This indicated that voters believed that Madison's administration had been good for the country. They were ready to keep his party in office by electing Monroe in November 1816. He had little opposition.

RETIREMENT. As he prepared to return to Montpelier as a retired statesman, John Adams gave him solid praise. Adams wrote that Madison's administration "notwithstanding a thousand faults & blunders has acquired more glory, & established more union, than all his three predecessors . . . put together."

In retirement, Madison remained intellectually active. Playing the role of elder statesman, the Sage of Montpelier entertained a steady stream of visitors. He became the president of the American Colonization Society, a group working to establish a republic in Africa as a refuge for freed American slaves. He was very aware of the need to follow Washington's example by granting freedom to the slaves at Montpelier, but his own financial problems prevented him from doing this. His most treasured asset was his notes on the Constitutional Convention of 1787, which he had decided not to publish while any of the Framers were still alive. Congress purchased the notes from his widow, and they appeared shortly after his own death. They provide a unique and invaluable insight into how his generation created a democratic republic. Madison was unwavering in his belief that the American experiment in self-government had become a beacon light for freedom-loving human beings everywhere. He died on 28 June 1836.

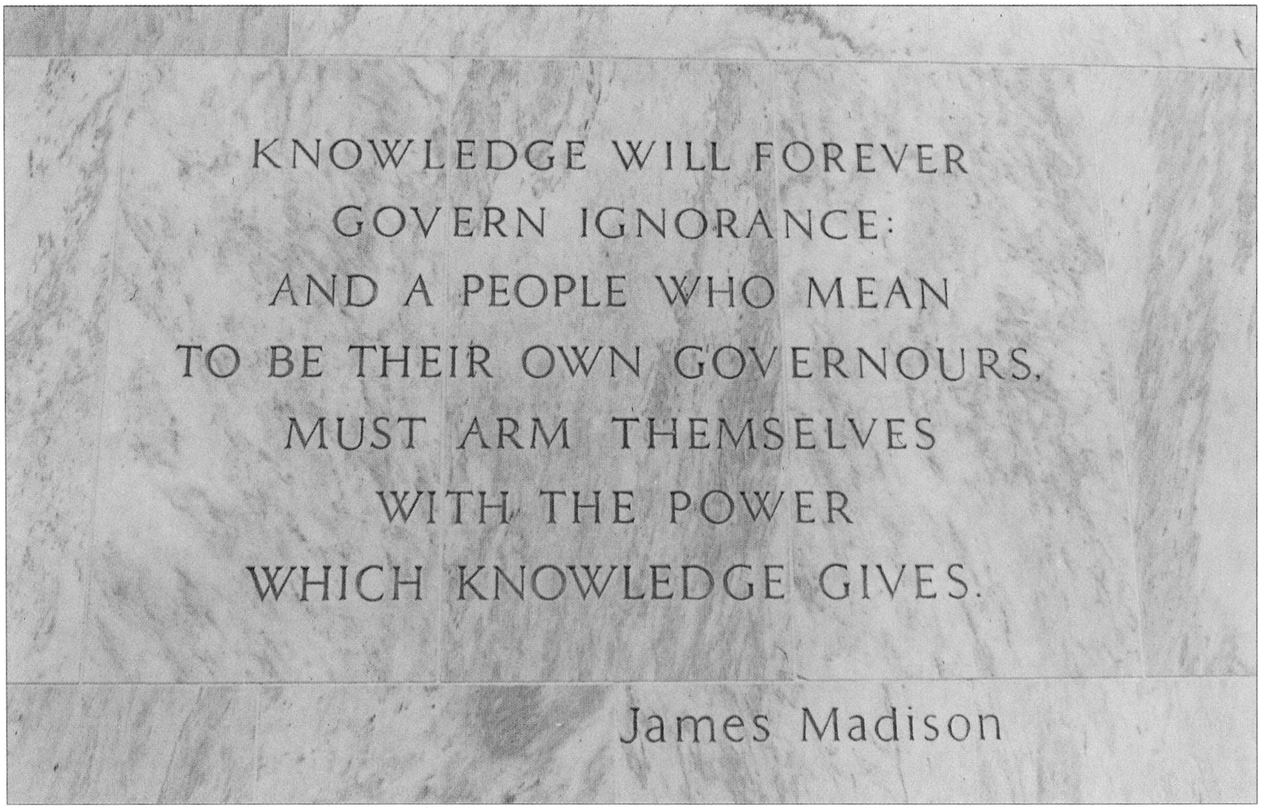

KNOWLEDGE WILL FOREVER
GOVERN IGNORANCE:
AND A PEOPLE WHO MEAN
TO BE THEIR OWN GOVERNOURS,
MUST ARM THEMSELVES
WITH THE POWER
WHICH KNOWLEDGE GIVES.

James Madison

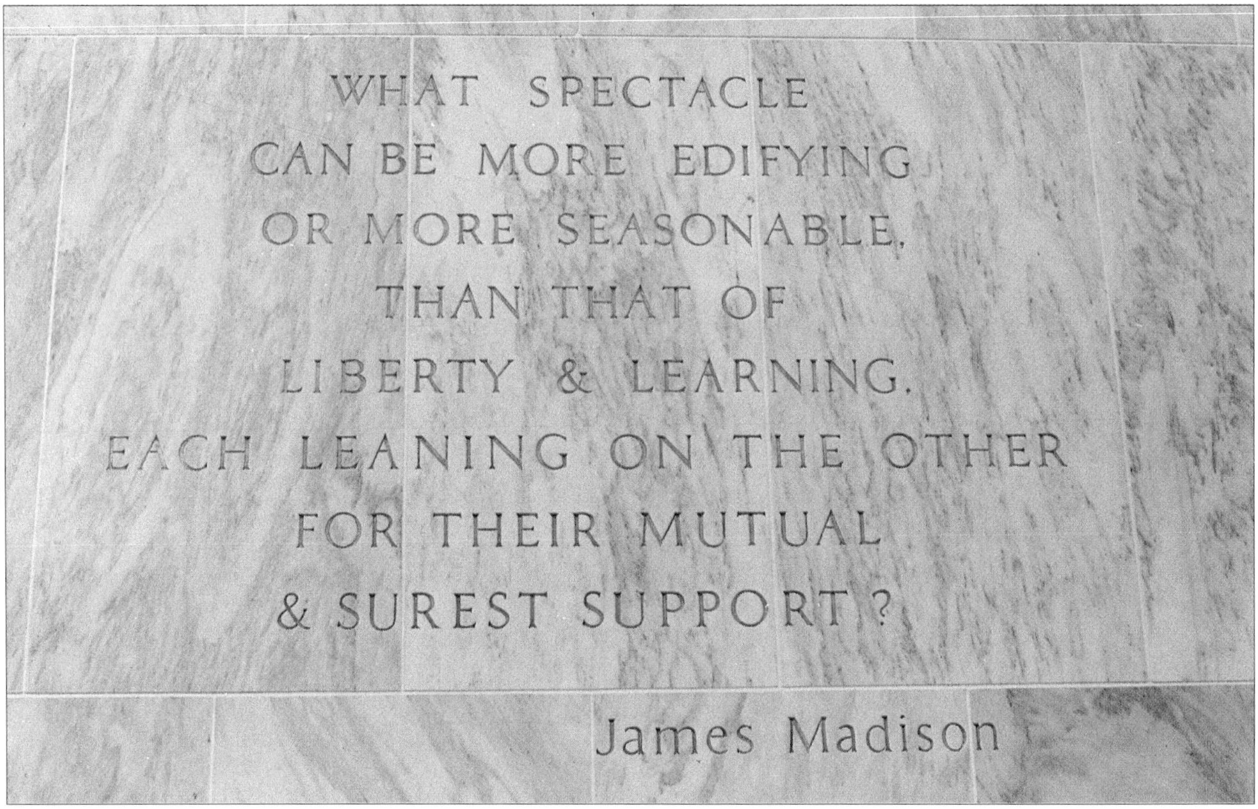

WHAT SPECTACLE
CAN BE MORE EDIFYING
OR MORE SEASONABLE,
THAN THAT OF
LIBERTY & LEARNING.
EACH LEANING ON THE OTHER
FOR THEIR MUTUAL
& SUREST SUPPORT?

James Madison

Quotations from a letter which Madison wrote to William T. Barry flank the entrance to the Madison Building, Library of Congress. Barry was postmaster general in President Andrew Jackson's cabinet.
(Photographs by Charles E. Smith.)

THOMAS JEFFERSON.   JAMES MADISON.   JOHN ADAMS.

This contemporary print placed James Madison with the three presidents who came before him. Madison left the presidency confident that the nation was in good shape. It was at peace and it was prosperous and expanding.

His eighth annual message to Congress, delivered on 3 December 1816, closed with farewell comments. He concluded by saying that he was leaving behind a government with "the most noble of all ambitions—that of promoting peace on earth and good will to man." (Courtesy Library of Congress.)

FAREWELL ADDRESS

. . . Happily, I shall carry with me from the public theater other sources, which those who love their country most will best appreciate. I shall behold it blessed with tranquillity and prosperity at home and with peace and respect abroad. I can indulge the proud reflection that the American people have reached in safety and success their fortieth year as an independent nation; that for nearly an entire generation they have had experience of their present Constitution, the offspring of their undisturbed deliberations and of their free choice; that they have found it to bear the trials of adverse as well as prosperous circumstances; to contain in its combination of the federate and elective principles a reconcilement of public strength with individual liberty, of national power for the defense of national rights with a security against wars of injustice, of ambition, and of vainglory in the fundamental provision which subjects all questions of war to the will of the nation itself, which is to pay its costs and feel its calamities. Nor is it less a peculiar felicity of this Constitution, so dear to us all, that it is found to be capable, without losing its vital energies, of expanding itself over a spacious territory with the increase and expansion of the community for whose benefit it was established. . . .

• *President James Madison delivered his Farewell Address (eighth annual message) to Congress on 3 December 1816.*

VICE PRESIDENT

George Clinton
(1739–1812)

CHRONOLOGICAL EVENTS

1739	Born, Little Britain, New York, 26 July
1759	Appointed clerk of common pleas for Ulster County
1765	Appointed district attorney
1768	Elected to New York State Assembly
1775	Elected to Second Continental Congress
1777	Served as brigadier general in the Continental army
1777	Elected governor of New York
1804	Elected vice president with Thomas Jefferson
1808	Elected vice president with James Madison
1812	Died, Washington, D.C., 20 April

BIOGRAPHY

By contrast to the polished Aaron Burr, Vice President George Clinton was neither an orator nor a skilled presiding officer. When Clinton first appeared in the U.S. Senate, his voice sounded so "weak & feeble" that few senators could understand him. He seemed uninformed about parliamentary procedure and uncomfortable when having to listen to long speeches. Ill health often kept him away from the Senate chamber. A widower, Clinton lived frugally in boarding houses, disliked Washington society, and rarely entertained. Ironically, his advanced age and poor health worked in his favor because other politicians no longer considered him competition.

Although Clinton was 69 years old in 1808, he still yearned to be president. When Madison received the presidential nomination, the Republican Caucus nominated Clinton for another term as vice president. Clinton's supporters denounced the Caucus, and Clinton neither accepted nor rejected renomination. Federalists — who had long opposed him — considered making Clinton their presidential candidate, but they concluded that his nomination would not persuade New York Republicans to bolt their party. Against his will, Clinton was reelected vice president. He did not bother to attend Madison's inauguration.

Clinton had grown increasingly hostile to the foreign policies of the Jefferson and Madison administrations. As a former governor of New York, Clinton opposed an embargo on U.S. goods to be shipped to warring nations in Europe because it would hurt New York merchants. He disapproved of the drift toward war with Great Britain, and he feared that the United States was not doing enough to prepare itself militarily.

Clinton also broke with Madison's domestic policies and aligned himself with the administration's opponents in the Senate. When Madison tried to recharter the national bank, Clinton cast the tie-breaking vote against it. Illness prevented him from becoming an effective leader of the administration's opposition or even from presiding much longer over the Senate. Clinton died in office in 1812 and became the first person honored by a state funeral in the U.S. Capitol. Although President Madison attended the funeral, he made little effort to mourn the vice president who had obstructed his policies and held his administration in such contempt.

VICE PRESIDENT

Elbridge Gerry
(1744–1814)

CHRONOLOGICAL EVENTS

1744   Born, Marblehead, Massachusetts, 17 July
1762   Graduated from Harvard College, Cambridge, Massachusetts
1776   Elected to Second Continental Congress
1787   Delegate to the Constitutional Convention
1788   Elected to U.S. House of Representatives
1797   Appointed special envoy to France
1810   Elected governor of Massachusetts
1812   Elected vice president
1814   Died, Washington, D.C., 23 November

BIOGRAPHY

The son of a prosperous merchant, Gerry attended Harvard before joining the family business. His opposition to British taxes won him election to the Massachusetts legislature. As a member of the Second Continental Congress, he signed the Declaration of Independence.

At the Constitutional Convention, Gerry chaired the committee that devised the "Great Compromise" between the large and the small states. Under this plan, membership in the U.S. House of Representatives was determined by population, while the states enjoyed equal representation in the U.S. Senate. Yet Gerry refused to sign the Constitution because it lacked a specific bill of rights.

Serving in the first House of Representatives, Gerry's support for Treasury Secretary Alexander Hamilton's financial programs identified him with the Federalists. In 1797, President John Adams made him a special envoy to France. That mission led to the so-called XYZ Affair. Three representatives of the French Government, known as X, Y, and Z, demanded bribes before they would negotiate. Federalist criticism of the mission pushed Gerry over to the opposition. In 1800, he backed Thomas Jefferson for president and became a leading Massachusetts Republican. Later, as governor of Massachusetts, he approved a controversial redistricting plan that created odd-shaped districts to give Republicans the advantage in elections. A Federalist cartoon of a salamander-shaped election district named it the "Gerrymander."

Although defeated for governor in 1812, Gerry was chosen to run for vice president with James Madison. In the U.S. Senate, he supported war with Great Britain, but opponents of the war held the majority. Gerry worried that with both himself and President Madison in ill health, the Senate might elect one of their opponents as president pro tempore (a temporary president who presided in the vice president's absence), who might then become president. Despite his ailments, Gerry presided every day to prevent the election of a president pro tempore.

Gerry was recuperating in Massachusetts during the summer of 1814 when British troops invaded Washington and burned the Capitol. He returned to preside over the Senate in temporary chambers in the Patent Office Building. His health continued to decline until he collapsed and died in his carriage on his way to preside over the Senate.

THE CABINET

SECRETARY OF STATE
Robert Smith, 1809
James Monroe, 1811, 1813

SECRETARY OF WAR
William Eustis, 1809
John Armstrong, 1813
James Monroe, 1814
William H. Crawford, 1815

SECRETARY OF THE TREASURY
Albert Gallatin, 1809, 1813
George W. Campbell, 1814
Alexander J. Dallas, 1814
William H. Crawford, 1816

POSTMASTER GENERAL
Gideon Granger, 1809, 1813
Return J. Meigs, Jr., 1814

ATTORNEY GENERAL
Caesar A. Rodney, 1809
William Pinckney, 1812, 1813
Richard Rush, 1814

SECRETARY OF THE NAVY
Robert Smith, 1809
Paul Hamilton, 1809
William Jones, 1813
Benjamin W. Crowninshield, 1814

(Courtesy Architect of the Capitol.)

Caesar A. Rodney (1772–1824). Rodney was a signer of the Declaration of Independence. He was appointed attorney general by President Thomas Jefferson in 1807.

After Aaron Burr was acquitted of treason for conspiring to have western states secede from the Union (1807), Rodney actively sought to broaden the legal definition of treason to include conspiracy. Reappointed by President James Madison in 1809, he was criticized for spending too much time with his law practice in Wilmington, Delaware. He resigned his post on 5 December 1811.

In 1823, President James Monroe appointed Rodney the first U.S. minister to the newly formed Argentine Republic. Shortly after arriving in Buenos Aires, he became ill and died.

FAMILY

CHRONOLOGICAL EVENTS

29 May 1768	Dolley Payne born	15 September 1794	Dolley Payne Todd married
1790	Dolley Payne married John Todd		James Madison
1793	John Todd died	28 June 1836	James Madison died
		12 July 1849	Dolley Madison died

(Courtesy Library of Congress.)

Dolley Madison's parents were Quakers; they freed their slaves and moved to Philadelphia from Virginia when she was a child. There she met and married a young Quaker lawyer. He died of yellow fever three years after their marriage. The epidemic which swept Philadelphia also claimed several in-laws and an infant son.

James Madison was 43 years old when he asked a mutual friend, Aaron Burr, to introduce him to the attractive young widow. They were married later that year. She was banished from her Quaker congregation because Madison was an Episcopalian, not a Quaker.

When her husband was appointed secretary of state, Dolley often acted as hostess for the widower President Thomas Jefferson. When her husband became president, she served as a gracious and charming First Lady. She remained in the White House as British troops were advancing on the city during the War of 1812. She stayed until the last minute to be sure that the portrait of George Washington by Gilbert Stuart was safely packed. This is the famous image that now appears on the one-dollar bill.

After Madison's death, she had to sell his papers, and the estate at Montpelier, including the slaves, furniture, and livestock. Her son, John Payne, was a heavy gambler, and she paid his debts on many occasions to keep him from going to prison. She remained at the core of Washington society until her death at 81.

MONTPELIER

Montpelier • P.O. Box 67 • Montpelier Station, Virginia 22957 • Tel: (703) 672-2728

James Madison was of the third generation of his family to live at Montpelier, a 2,700-acre estate located in the lush Piedmont of Virginia. (Courtesy Montpelier, 1994. National Trust for Historic Preservation. Photograph by Philip Beaurline.)

Located approximately 25 miles north of Charlottesville. Open daily, March through December, from 10 A.M. to 4 P.M.; January through February, open weekends only, from 10 A.M. to 4 P.M. Closed first Saturday in November, Thanksgiving, Christmas, and New Year's Day. Admission fee includes a bus tour of the 2,700-acre estate and a tour of the mansion. Administered by the National Trust for Historic Preservation.

In 1723, James Madison's grandfather, Ambrose, received a patent of land in what is now Orange County, Virginia. The estate prospered under the ownership of Madison's parents, James, Sr. and Nelly. The original brick mansion, completed around 1765, probably was designed and built by Madison's father. In 1794, Madison married Dolley Payne Todd, and they then lived at Montpelier with his mother.

Between 1797 and 1800, Madison significantly renovated the mansion's exterior to include a 30-foot addition to the northeast end of the house plus a front porch; between 1809 and 1812, he ordered interior renovations (including the Madison dining room) as well as the construction of one-story wings to each end of the house. During these renovations, the kitchens were brought inside the main house.

After the completion of his second presidential term, Madison retired to Montpelier and lived there until his death in 1836. Following his death, the contents of the mansion were auctioned off, and his wife returned to Washington, D.C., where she died in 1849. The estate changed hands six times until 1900, when it was purchased by William and Anna Roger duPont, who enlarged the mansion and added stables, greenhouses, a dairy, and a railroad station. In 1928, their daughter, Marion duPont Scott, took over the property and added a steeplechase track. After her death in 1983, the National Trust for Historic Preservation received the property. In 1987, it was opened to the public as part of the celebration of the bicentennial of the United States Constitution.

THE OCTAGON

1799 New York Avenue, NW
Washington, D.C. 20006-5292
Tel: (202) 638-3221

On 17 February 1815, President James Madison signed the Treaty of Ghent in the upstairs parlor of The Octagon, five months after the British burned the White House.
(Photograph by Charles E. Smith.) ▶

Located at Eighteenth Street and New York Avenue, can be reached via the Metro orange and blue lines to Farragut West station (18th and I streets). Open Tuesday through Sunday from 10 A.M. to 4 P.M. Closed Thanksgiving, Christmas, and New Year's Day. Admission fee. Administered by The American Architectural Foundation.

The Octagon was completed in 1801 for the prominent Tayloe family. It was designed by William Thornton, the original architect of the U.S. Capitol. After the British burned the White House during the War of 1812, Colonel John Tayloe, a wealthy Virginia planter, offered his townhouse to President Madison and his wife, Dolley. The Madisons lived there for nearly a year, from 1814 to 1815. They then moved to one of the "Seven Buildings," a series of attached townhouses built along Pennsylvania Avenue in 1796. They lived there for the remainder of the President's term in office.

After 1855, the Tayloe family no longer lived in the house. In 1865, the St. Rose's Technical Institute occupied the house, and from 1866 to 1879, the government rented it for the use of the Hydrographic Office. The American Institute of Architects took possession of the building in 1898 and purchased it in 1902. It is administered by The American Architectural Foundation, which hosts internationally renowned exhibitions on architecture and design.

When British troops burned the Capitol in August 1814, the collection of the Library of Congress, consisting of several hundred volumes, was destroyed. Thomas Jefferson wrote to President Madison offering his personal library of more than 6 thousand volumes and, with Madison's approval, they were brought to Washington. This was the beginning of one of the greatest libraries in the world. It contains more than 60 million items.

A statue of Madison, sculpted by Walter K. Hancock, is located on the first floor of the James Madison Memorial Building, the third and newest of the three buildings of the Library of Congress. This building was opened in 1980. (Photograph by Charles E. Smith.) ▶

93

James Monroe

5TH PRESIDENT
OF THE UNITED STATES OF AMERICA

CHRONOLOGICAL EVENTS

28 April 1758	Born, Westmoreland County, Virginia
25–26 December 1776	Wounded in Battle of Trenton, New Jersey
1779	Studied law on advice of Virginia Governor Thomas Jefferson
June 1780	Appointed military commissioner with rank of lieutenant colonel
1782	Elected to Virginia Assembly
June 1783	Elected to Continental Congress, served 3 terms
October 1786	Admitted to bar, Fredericksburg, Virginia
2 June 1788	Elected to Virginia state convention which ratified the U.S. Constitution
November 1790	Elected to U.S. Senate
May 1794	Appointed U.S. minister to France
22 August 1796	Recalled from France
December 1797	Wrote *A View of the Conduct of the Executive in the Foreign Affairs of the United States*
5 December 1799	Elected governor of Virginia
12 January 1803	Appointed special envoy to France
18 April 1803	Appointed U.S. minister to Great Britain
30 April 1803	Signed treaty with France transferring Louisiana to the United States
12 July 1803	Arrived in London, England
1804	Led diplomatic mission to Spain
1806	Negotiated Monroe-Pinkney Treaty with Great Britain
December 1807	Returned to the United States
1810	Elected to Virginia House of Delegates
January –March 1811	Served as governor of Virginia
2 April 1811	Appointed secretary of state
27 September 1814	Appointed secretary of war
1816	Elected president
4 March 1817	Inaugurated president
1817	Toured northeastern states
25 February 1819	Approved Adams-Onis Treaty with Spain
1820	Reelected president
5 March 1821	Inaugurated president
4 May 1822	Vetoed Cumberland Road Bill
2 December 1823	Announced Monroe Doctrine
1829	Elected chair at the Virginia Constitutional Convention
4 July 1831	Died, New York, New York

BIOGRAPHY

James Monroe was born on his parents' 600-acre plantation in Westmoreland County, Virginia, on 28 April 1758. He was still a student at William and Mary College when the American Revolution began in 1776. Monroe left the classroom and was commissioned a lieutenant in a Virginia volunteer regiment. He served at the battles of Harlem Heights and White Plains, then was severely wounded at the Battle of Trenton. He also saw action at the battles of Brandywine, Germantown, and Monmouth. In 1778, he was promoted to the rank of lieutenant colonel before his 20th birthday. Monroe was at Valley Forge during the terrible winter of 1778, awaiting a command. Because of his close physical resemblance to George Washington, Monroe was sometimes mistaken for his commanding general.

Ordered back to Virginia to help raise a new regiment, Monroe met Governor Thomas Jefferson who sensed an uncommon talent for leadership in the young officer. Jefferson encouraged Monroe to study law and to seek a seat in the Virginia Assembly, to which Monroe was elected in 1782. Jefferson also introduced Monroe to James Madison. The three men were to work closely together for many years. In addition, Monroe had help from his uncle, Joseph Jones, an influential member of the Continental Congress who was pleased when his nephew was added to the Virginia delegation to the Congress in 1783.

In 1786, while in Congress, Monroe met and married Elizabeth Kortright, the daughter of a once-prosperous New York merchant. Monroe returned to Virginia, and in 1788, allied himself

George Washington at the Battle of Trenton. James Monroe was promoted to major for bravery in action at this battle, where he was wounded. (Courtesy National Archives.)

with Patrick Henry and the forces opposed to ratification of the Constitution. He started a law practice in Fredericksburg and was urged by Henry to run for a seat in the first Federal Congress against his old friend, James Madison. Monroe lost the election in a friendly contest.

Henry, still a major force in Virginia politics, soon was responsible for Monroe being elected to the U. S. Senate. There Monroe became part of the circle of Jefferson's friends who opposed the Federalist programs of Alexander Hamilton, who increasingly dominated the policy-making machine in Washington's administration. Monroe impressed his Senate colleagues with his honesty and his personality. In February 1791, Monroe proposed that the Senate end its policy of debating in secret, but his proposal to open the Senate doors was defeated, 17 to 9.

U.S. MINISTER TO FRANCE. President Washington sent Monroe to Paris as the U.S. minister in 1794. One of the chief quarrels between Jefferson and Alexander Hamilton had

James Monroe held more major offices than any other president. He was a U.S. senator; governor of Virginia; minister to Great Britain, France, and Spain; secretary of state; secretary of war; and president of the United States. (Courtesy Library of Congress.)

been over the direction taken by the French Revolution. Monroe, like Jefferson, was sympathetic toward the original high goals of the French Revolution. However, he arrived in Paris soon after the Reign of Terror had changed the Revolution's course. French leaders were convinced that U.S. policy favored the British in the raging Anglo-French War. An improvement in Franco-American relations depended on how the French understood Washington's policy toward Great Britain. When the provisions of Jay's Treaty in 1795 were revealed, the French became even more certain that U.S. policy was pro-British and anti-French. Thereafter, Monroe's task became more difficult. In 1796, he was recalled because Secretary of State Timothy Pickering thought Monroe was too friendly with the French.

While the Federalists were in power, Jefferson wrote both Madison and Monroe, suggesting that they should aim for the presidency—a wish that he lived to see fulfilled. Jefferson once told a friend that Monroe was an exceptional person, "Turn his soul wrong side outwards and there is not a speck on it." At the time, however, both Madison and Monroe denied having any presidential ambitions and supported Jefferson as the Democratic-Republican candidate in the 1796 election. Jefferson lost this election to John Adams by only three electoral votes.

Back in his native Virginia, Monroe purchased a 2,500-acre plantation near Jefferson's Monticello estate. Although he was in debt, like many Virginians of his time, he bought more land on credit. He later bought a large estate, Oak Hill, in Loudoun County, Virginia. Monroe was paying several mortgages at once and needed income desperately. He had to sell some of the French furniture he had brought back from Paris in order to pay current bills. In such circumstances, Monroe was reconsidering opening a private law practice when the state legislature elected him governor of Virginia, a post he would hold from 1800 to 1803.

The presidential election of 1800 went to the U.S. House of Representatives for a final resolution. Governor Monroe was among those ready to

send troops into the capital when it appeared that the forces behind Aaron Burr were threatening a coup d'état (overthrow of the government). The threats proved overblown and finally Jefferson was declared the winner late in February 1801. Once in office, Jefferson sent Monroe back to Paris as a special envoy. He joined Robert R. Livingston and helped negotiate the Louisiana Purchase in 1803. Dazzled by that success, Jefferson named Monroe the U.S. minister to Great Britain.

Monroe's new task proved to be hopeless. In negotiations with the British foreign minister, he sought to resolve Anglo-American disputes over the rights of neutral ships in wartime. In 1806, Monroe and special envoy William Pinkney signed an agreement in which the British gave up little. Regarding the impressment (illegal capture) of U.S. sailors, the British diplomats insisted that the Royal Navy had a legal right to search for deserters but promised that in the future "the strictest care shall be taken to preserve the citizens of the United States from any molestation or injury." In other words, they left impressment where it was when they started. Monroe and Pinkney believed that the treaty they finally obtained was favorable. They felt that the statement on impressment, weak as it was, might stop the Royal Navy's seizure of sailors on U.S. ships. Jefferson, however, was displeased with the Monroe-Pinkney Treaty and never sent it to the U.S. Senate for ratification.

A DISAPPOINTED DIPLOMAT. After his return to the United States late in 1807, Monroe was disappointed to learn of the treaty's fate. He was also upset because Jefferson did not discuss his political future when they met in the White House. On a more personal level, Monroe became less friendly with his old friend, Secretary of State James Madison, whom Monroe blamed for the treaty's failure.

In 1808, some Republicans wanted to nominate Monroe for the presidency, even though it was well known that James Madison was Jefferson's choice for the nomination. Monroe was nominated by congressmen who were critical of Jefferson, despite the regular Republicans' selection of Madison a few days before. Jefferson, during his last weeks in the White House, wrote Monroe of his disappointment: "I have ever viewed Mr. Madison and yourself as [the] two principal pillars of my happiness." The gesture helped heal Monroe's wounded feelings. Madison won the national election in a landslide.

Monroe accepted the possibility that his public service career might have ended. He borrowed $10,000 to improve his farms and bought slaves to work his Albemarle County property, known then as Highlands.

An improvement in Monroe's relations with President Madison came in spring 1810, when he went to Washington to press his claims for back pay. Madison invited him to the White House and extended to him the hand of friendship. Monroe wrote a long public letter explaining why he had permitted his nomination in 1808 in opposition to Madison. Monroe ran against Madison with no hope of winning, but he felt that the contest would help heal his hurt feelings.

Elected to the Virginia House of Delegates, Monroe was back in Richmond in fall 1810 when Governor John Tyler resigned to accept a federal judgeship. A movement to elect Monroe governor almost collapsed because party regulars questioned his loyalty. However, in January 1811, Monroe was chosen to serve as Virginia's chief executive. Monroe's service as governor was brief. In March 1811, President Madison fired his secretary of state and offered the post to Monroe.

SECRETARY OF STATE. Monroe accepted and threw himself into the very difficult situation that that Anglo-American diplomatic relations had become. President Madison wanted the British to withdraw their Orders in Council, a device used by the Royal Navy to justify the seizure of U.S. sailors and goods at sea. Madison insisted that U.S. neutrality be recognized, and Monroe defended Madison's policy.

Thus, the two old friends worked to avoid war with Great Britain until the final break came in spring 1812. Madison had fallen into a French diplomatic trap and reopened commerce with the French. In fact, the French continued to seize U.S. ships. In his embarrassment, Monroe summoned the French minister to protest the dishonesty. "The Administration finds itself in the most extreme embarrassment," Monroe told the French diplomat, unless Napoleon would do what he promised, and quickly.

The British and the French engaged in a shouting match over who was violating what. With Monroe by his side, Madison played his last card. Either the British would withdraw their Orders and stop interfering with U.S. shipping, or the gravest consequences would follow. The British minister in Washington thought all this talk from Madison and Monroe was a bluff and told his superiors in London that they could ignore the Yankee threat.

WAR OF 1812. As Monroe and Madison soon learned, nothing had changed in the British cabinet's official attitude. Upon hearing this, Madison's patience was exhausted, and he sent a war message to Congress. Congress declared war on Great Britain in June 1812. Much loose talk was heard in Congress about a quick and easy invasion of Canada that would be followed by a negotiated settlement with Great Britain, but the sudden loss of Detroit to British troops stopped such talk.

Madison knew little of military matters and depended on Monroe for counsel as he surveyed the Detroit disaster. Monroe himself was frustrated, for he saw a military career as a better way to advance than the State Department. At one time, Madison had considered making Monroe the commander of a U.S. force that would attack key Canadian targets for a swift victory. However, that plan was changed when western congressmen wanted William Henry Harrison to lead an invading army.

Once reelected in 1812, Madison fired his inefficient secretary of war, William Eustis, and called on Monroe to assume a second cabinet post. However, the Senate refused to confirm Monroe, mainly because he was from Virginia. So Madison made Monroe acting secretary of war and kept seeking a qualified permanent war secretary. Meanwhile, Monroe took charge of the War Department, issued orders for troop enlistments, and drafted plans for a spring offensive in 1813.

HOLDS TWO CABINET POSTS. Monroe still thought it was possible to invade Canada and asked for a 30,000-man army. Congress voted Monroe the funds and authorized the manpower. Madison had found a replacement for his acting secretary, and after 10 weeks, Monroe went back to the State Department and left John Armstrong in charge of running the war. Unfortunately, Armstrong was not equipped for the job despite his military background. He sidetracked plans to give Monroe command of an invasion army and instead tried to give him a subordinate post as a brigadier general. Monroe turned down the job and stayed at the State Department.

Madison eagerly seized the offer of Tsar Alexander I of Russia to mediate an end to the Anglo-American war. Monroe had his own list of peace commissioners, but he yielded to Madison's choices. After some delay, the U.S. diplomats settled down in the Belgian city of Ghent to negotiate an end to the war.

The land war continued to be an embarrassment to the United States. Armstrong failed at his job, as did senior commanders in the field. With a few exceptions the U.S. invasion of Canada turned into a complete failure leaving behind damaged reputations and several thousand U.S. casualties.

In August 1814, British marines marched into Washington almost untouched, burned several public buildings (including the White House), and withdrew after their powder magazine exploded. Monroe had been with the President, inspecting the capital's defenses, before the militia forces collapsed. As a complete defeat became evident, Monroe found the President and his party on the outskirts of Washington. He then rushed back to try and stiffen the resolve of retreating Americans. Madison called for his cabinet, so Monroe left the field of battle and was with the President when the decision to flee the capital was made.

Three days after the British left Washington, Monroe accompanied President Madison as several cabinet members returned to view the results. Disgusted with Armstrong's performance, Madison hinted that his resignation would be accepted, and once again Monroe found himself holding two cabinet posts. As secretary of war, Monroe focused his attention on Baltimore, where a British force was defeated on 14 September.

When news of the peace treaty arrived from Ghent, Monroe was still involved in planning a defense force in preparation for a longer war that included a draft and an army of 100,000 men. Then came news of General Andrew Jackson's victory at New Orleans on 8 January 1815. This was followed by official dispatches confirming a peace treaty. Monroe handed them to Madison on 14 February. A Baltimore newspaper headline told the story: "Glorious News! Orleans Saved and Peace Concluded." Madison and his cabinet received congratulations as the news spread, but Monroe was thinking about the failures of the previous fall. Before he left the War Department in March 1815, he wrote a report recommending a peacetime military force and a large budget for improved coastal defenses. Monroe suffered from an illness, but he had regained his weight and was feeling better by mid-summer. Hushed conversation on Capitol Hill left no doubt that the congressional caucus early in 1816 would chose Monroe as the Republican presidential nominee.

Before Monroe was involved in partisan politics, however, there was unfinished business left over from the war. Working with British Minister Sir Charles Bagot in Washington, Monroe helped secure an agreement in 1816 for the demilitarization of the Great Lakes. The formal treaty was not ratified until 1818, but the disarmament of the U.S.–Canadian border was a fact before Monroe left the State Department early in 1817.

ELECTION OF 1816. Although President Madison had never publicly endorsed Monroe as

FIRST INAUGURAL ADDRESS

. . . From the commencement of our Revolution to the present day almost forty years have elapsed, and from the establishment of this Constitution twenty-eight. Through this whole term the government has been what may emphatically be called self-government. And what has been the effect? To whatever object we turn our attention, whether it relates to our foreign or domestic concerns, we find abundant cause to felicitate ourselves in the excellence of our institutions. During a period fraught with difficulties and marked by very extraordinary events the United States have flourished beyond example. Their citizens individually have been happy and the nation prosperous.

Under this Constitution our commerce has been wisely regulated with foreign nations and between the states; new states have been admitted into our Union; our territory has been enlarged by fair and honorable treaty, and with great advantage to the original states; the states, respectively protected by the national government under a mild, parental system against foreign dangers, and enjoying within their separate spheres, by a wise partition of power, a just proportion of the sovereignty, have improved their police, extended their settlements, and attained a strength and maturity which are the best proofs of wholesome laws well administered. And if we look to the condition of individuals what a proud spectacle does it exhibit! On whom has oppression fallen in any quarter of our Union? Who has been deprived of any right of person or property? Who restrained from offering his vows in the mode which he prefers to the Divine Author of his being? It is well known that all these blessings have been enjoyed in their fullest extent; and I add with peculiar satisfaction that there has been no example of a capital punishment being inflicted on anyone for the crime of high treason.

Some who might admit the competency of our government to these beneficent duties might doubt it in trials which put to the test its strength and efficiency as a member of the great community of nations. Here too experience has afforded us the most satisfactory proof in its favor. Just as this Constitution was put into action several of the principal states of Europe had become much agitated and some of them seriously convulsed. Destructive wars ensued, which have of late only been terminated. In the course of these conflicts the United States received great injury from several of the parties. It was their interest to stand aloof from the contest, to demand justice from the party committing the injury, and to cultivate by a fair and honorable conduct the friendship of all. War became at length inevitable, and the result has shown that our government is equal to that, the greatest of trials, under the most unfavorable circumstances. Of the virtue of the people and of the heroic exploits of the army, the navy, and the militia I need not speak. . . .

• *On 4 March 1817, the inaugural ceremonies took place outside for the first time since 1789. Monroe had informed the U.S. Senate that, according to custom, he would take the presidential oath in the chamber of the U.S. House of Representatives. A dispute arose, however, between the Senate and the House inaugural committees. To settle the matter, an elevated portico (porch) was constructed in front of the Capitol. From there, Monroe repeated the oath of office and delivered his inaugural address to "an immense concourse (gathering) of officers of the Government, foreign officers, strangers, and citizens."*

his successor, Republican leaders in Congress knew that Monroe was eager for the post. Only William H. Crawford, a cabinet member and a popular senator from Georgia, and Governor Daniel Tompkins of New York presented a challenge in the congressional caucus that was to decide the Republican nominee. There was resentment, particularly in the New York delegation, against the "Virginia dynasty" label—only John Adams had broken the Virginia hold on the presidency since 1789. But no coalition or alliance could stop Monroe, who was the last of the Revolutionary generation to stand in line for the presidency. In the March 1816 caucus, Monroe received 65 votes to Crawford's 54.

The Federalists were so disorganized that their candidate, Rufus King, was defeated badly everywhere except in New England when the general election was held. In the electoral college, Monroe received 183 votes while King received only 34 votes. The New York Democratic Republicans pushed Governor Daniel Tompkins into the second place on the ticket. Tompkins presided over the Senate as vice president until 1825.

After Monroe's inauguration on 4 March 1817, he made his cabinet choices with skill. He chose John Quincy Adams as secretary of state, made Crawford secretary of the treasury, and after several turndowns, he convinced John C. Calhoun to become secretary of war. The minor cabinet posts were filled by holdovers from Madison's administration, and the harmony that prevailed under Monroe contrasted sharply with the continuous arguing that had marked Madison's first years in office.

PANIC OF 1819. Peacetime America experienced a period of prosperity until the panic of 1819 struck and left a wake of bankruptcy, depressed farm prices, and personal ruin. Wildcat banking practices and runaway land speculation triggered the panic, which saw the debts owed the government on public land purchases rose from $3 million in 1815 to $22 million in 1819. In spring 1819, paper money might be worth a dollar in gold from a sound bank or almost worthless if issued by a weak state-chartered bank. The further south one traveled, the worse the currency became. In fact, a popular saying at that time was that money was so cheap, counterfeiting was hardly worthwhile.

ERA OF GOOD FEELING. Before the panic of 1819, Monroe had visited the middle and northern states on a goodwill tour in 1817. At that time, a Boston newspaper editor hailed Monroe's new administration as ushering in "an era of good feeling." Indeed, Monroe wanted the bitterness of party warfare ended. His welcome in New England by old enemies marked at least the end of the Federalists' hostility. Political infighting within the Republican Party was bound to occur, but Monroe was pleased to see that by the middle of his first administration, all of New England except Massachusetts had Republican leadership. The Federalist ranks in Congress were substantially reduced. Renominated for the presidency by the congressional caucus in 1820, Monroe made no campaign effort in what became an election without a contest. Virtually unopposed, Monroe became president-elect almost by default. In the electoral college, he won all the votes but one—cast for John Quincy Adams by an angry New Englander.

Monroe found himself in conflict with Henry Clay when the Kentuckian pushed through Congress a bill offering government aid for the construction of the Cumberland Road to the West. In 1818, the road had reached Wheeling in western Virginia, from which passengers and freight could be transported on the Ohio River. Clay rallied his supporters, and in 1822, they passed an extension bill that committed the federal government to a plan involving tolls and maintenance of a national highway. Monroe was mindful that his predecessors, Jefferson and Madison, believed in the "strict construction" of the Constitution and vetoed the bill on the grounds that it was unconstitutional. Meanwhile, the panic of 1819 had lessened enthusiasm for internal improvements aided by the federal government. The Erie Canal,

Although President Monroe was inaugurated on 4 March 1817, he and his wife did not move into the President's House until September. The building had been burned by the British during the War of 1812. It was renovated and painted and was known as the White House thereafter. (Courtesy National Archives.)

finished during Monroe's second term, had been built by New York State without federal aid, but western states, according to Clay, needed federal help. Monroe did not agree with Clay.

Guided by Secretary of State John Quincy Adams, President Monroe achieved several major triumphs in foreign affairs. The Spanish occupation of Florida had long been a problem to southerners. Constant guerrilla warfare along the Georgia-Florida border was carried out by renegade Seminoles who offered a refuge to runaway slaves. This ended when the United States purchased the territory, confirmed by the Adams-Onis treaty early in 1819. General Andrew Jackson's invasion of Florida in 1818 to punish the Seminole warriors had frightened the Spanish. They realized that the United States could seize that region whenever it wished. Monroe supported Adams's careful diplomatic approach. The Spanish minister agreed to sell Florida, but saved Texas for his king.

THE MONROE DOCTRINE. Far more important, perhaps, was the warning Monroe gave in his annual message to Congress on 2 December 1823. At that time, he told European nations that the western continents were "not to be considered as subjects for future colonization by any European powers." Years of diplomatic maneuvering preceded Monroe's pronouncement. In 1821, Tsar Alexander I had claimed for Russia a coastal strip from Alaska south toward the U.S. border. Adams rejected that claim at once. He said that the United States was committed to the principle that the American continents "are no longer subjects of any new European colonial establishments." The more immediate cause of Monroe's statement was the confusion in Latin America caused by rebellions in every province claimed by a crumbling Spanish empire. Spain resented the efforts of its rebellious colonies to gain recognition as independent states, and it warned its European neighbors not to interfere. Spain itself was having a problem at that time. Its so-called constitutional government had captured King

Ferdinand VII and was holding him prisoner. The French intervened and when Ferdinand regained nominal control, he insisted on recapturing the rebellious provinces. It was an empty threat. In addition, the British were interested in the future of Latin America as a market for the growing industrial output of its mills and factories.

Monroe's secretary of state, John Quincy Adams, was convinced that the Spanish were powerless to regain their former possessions in the Americas. However, he was worried about Cuba, where Spain remained in power. Adams feared that Great Britain might occupy the "pearl of the Caribbean." He instructed the U.S. minister in London to determine the British attitude toward Cuba. Monroe was assured that the British wanted no outside interference in the Spanish colonies that were in revolt. Monroe asked his cabinet for guidance regarding a joint Anglo-American declaration warning European powers to stay out of South America. Adams opposed the idea because it might require the United States to give up of any hope of ever acquiring Cuba or Texas. This advice from Adams influenced Monroe, who in his final draft of the Monroe Doctrine confined his warning to "any European power." At the time, the Spanish and the French both pretended to be unimpressed by Monroe's powerful statement. The Monroe Doctrine grew into a permanent fixture of U.S. foreign policy.

MISSOURI COMPROMISE. Slavery was no easier to handle in Monroe's time than it had been in previous administrations. Sectional tensions were temporarily overcome with a congressional compromise over the admission of Missouri as a slave state in 1820, but Missouri's southern boundary (36°30') was set as the northern limits for the extension of slavery in western territories. Monroe remained essentially an interested spectator during the battle in Congress, but his sympathies were with the compromisers led by Senator Henry Clay. Monroe's only involvement came when the electoral count for the 1820 election was announced by the president of the Senate and angry southern senators wanted Missouri's votes recorded. A week

MONROE DOCTRINE

. . . As a principle in which the rights and interests of the United States are involved, that the American continents, by the free and independent condition which they have assumed and maintain, are henceforth not to be considered as subjects for future colonization by any European powers. . . .

In the wars of the European powers in matters relating to themselves we have never taken any part, nor does it comport with our policy so to do. It is only when our rights are invaded or seriously menaced that we resent injuries or make preparation for our defense. With the movements in this hemisphere we are of necessity more immediately connected, and by causes which must be obvious to all enlightened and impartial observers. The political system of the allied powers is essentially different in this respect from that of America. . . . We owe it, therefore, to candor and to the amicable relations existing between the United States and those powers to declare that we should consider any attempt on their part to extend their system to any portion of this hemisphere as dangerous to our peace and safety. With the existing colonies or dependencies of any European power we have not interfered and shall not interfere. But with the Governments who have declared their independence and maintained it, and whose independence we have, on great consideration and on just principles, acknowledged, we could not view any interposition for the purpose of oppressing them, or controlling in any other manner their destiny, by any European power in any other light than as the manifestation of an unfriendly disposition toward the United States. In the war between those new Governments and Spain we declared our neutrality at the time of their recognition, and to this we have adhered, and shall continue to adhere, provided no change shall occur which, in the judgment of the competent authorities of this Government, shall make a corresponding change on the part of the United States indispensable to their security. . . .

Our policy in regard to Europe. . . remains the same, which is, not to interfere in the internal concerns of any of its powers; to consider the government de facto as the legitimate government for us; to cultivate friendly relations with it, and to preserve those relations by a frank, firm, and manly policy, meeting in all instances the just claims of every power, submitting to injuries from none. But in regard to those continents circumstances are eminently and conspicuously different. It is impossible that the allied powers should extend their political system to any portion of either continent without endangering our peace and happiness; nor can anyone believe that our southern brethren, if left to themselves, would adopt it of their own accord. It is equally impossible, therefore, that we should behold such interposition in any form with indifference. . . .

• *The paragraphs on foreign policy in President Monroe's Seventh Annual Message (2 December 1823) are referred to as the Monroe Doctrine. It contained four main provisions—two warnings and two assurances to European nations: 1) The United States would oppose further extension or colonization of European nations in the Western Hemisphere; 2) The United States would oppose any interference by European nations in the internal affairs of any Western Hemisphere country; 3) The United States would not interfere in the existing Western Hemisphere colonies of any European nation; 4) The United States would not become involved in the internal affairs of any European nation.*

Monroe's message drew little attention from the nations of Europe. The Doctrine is important, however, because it clearly and concisely summarizes U.S. foreign policy.

EIGHTH ANNUAL MESSAGE

. . . Our institutions form an important epoch in the history of the civilized world. On their preservation and in their utmost purity everything will depend. Extending as our interests do to every part of the inhabited globe and to every sea to which our citizens are carried by their industry and enterprise, to which they are invited by the wants of others, and have a right to go, we must either protect them in the enjoyment of their rights or abandon them in certain events to waste and desolation. Our attitude is highly interesting as relates to other powers, and particularly to our southern neighbors. We have duties to perform with respect to all to which we must be faithful. To every kind of danger we should pay the most vigilant and unceasing attention, remove the cause where it may be practicable, and be prepared to meet it when inevitable.

Against foreign danger the policy of the government seems to be already settled. The events of the late war admonished us to make our maritime frontier impregnable by a well digested chain of fortifications, and to give efficient protection to our commerce by augmenting our navy to a certain extent, which has been steadily pursued, and which it is incumbent upon us to complete as soon as circumstances will permit. In the event of war it is on the maritime frontier that we shall be assailed. It is in that quarter, therefore, that we should be prepared to meet the attack. It is there that our whole force will be called into action to prevent the destruction of our towns and the desolation and pillage of the interior. To give full effect to this policy great improvements will be indispensable. Access to those works by every practicable communication should be made easy and in every direction. . . .

• *The administrations of James Monroe (1817–1825) settled boundary disputes with Canada (1818), acquired Florida from Spain (1819), and formulated the Monroe Doctrine (1823). In his last annual message to Congress (7 December 1824), Monroe seems to support the continued economic, political, and territorial expansion of the United States: "We have duties to perform with respect to all to which we must be faithful."*

---

later, on 22 February 1821, Clay engineered the creation of a joint committee of Congress that resolved the dispute and instructed the President to proclaim Missouri's statehood "to be considered as complete." Monroe did as Congress ordered and proclaimed Missouri a part of the Union on 10 August 1821. A generation would pass before the settlement was questioned. A civil war had to be fought to reach the ultimate solution.

Monroe's final years in the White House were marked by a decline in government revenues, a tightening of the federal budget, and sharp infighting among Republicans who wanted to succeed Monroe in the 1824 election. A severe illness harmed Crawford's chances, and Monroe's role in securing victory for John Quincy Adams over Andrew Jackson in the presidential contest was minimal.

RETIREMENT. Long accustomed to debts, Monroe was able to save nothing from his $25,000 annual salary as president. In retirement at his northern Virginia plantation, Monroe attended to his wife's health and struggled with debts of some $75,000. He sent claims for past expenses during his diplomatic missions, and Congress approved a $29,513 payment in 1826. In 1828, Monroe was injured in a fall from a horse but recovered enough to attend the 1829 Virginia constitutional convention in Richmond in the company of Madison and John Marshall. As one of

This statue stands in the garden at Ash Lawn-Highland outside Charlottesville, Virginia. Monroe had hoped to retire to this estate but his personal finances and the death of his wife, Elizabeth, prevented that. (Courtesy A. A. M. van der Heyden.)

CEREMONY

OF THE

DISINTERMENT

AND

REMOVAL

FROM THE CITY OF NEW YORK

SIC SEMPER TYRANNIS

OF

THE REMAINS

OF

JAMES MONROE

PRESIDENT

OF THE UNITED STATES

A.D. 1817—1825

to VIRGINIA,

his native State

July 1858

Tribute to his memory by Virginians
and their descendants in New York.

Lith by HATCH & Co. 91 William St N.Y.

his last public acts, Monroe served as president of the convention and in the debate sought to moderate the conflict over slavery and representation for the western counties.

Poor health forced Monroe to retire from his post at the convention. He returned to Oak Hill and was broken hearted by his wife's death in September 1830. He moved to New York to live with his daughter, Maria Gouverneur, and her family. His health declined further. Congress, touched by the poverty and illness of the fading Founding Father, voted another $30,000 for his debt claims. He died on 4 July 1831.

James Monroe moved to New York to live with his daughter, Maria Gouverneur. He died there on 4 July 1831. In July 1858, his remains were removed to Richmond, Virginia.
(Courtesy Collection David J. and Janice L. Frent.)

VICE PRESIDENT

Daniel D. Tompkins
(1774–1825)

CHRONOLOGICAL EVENTS

1774	Born, Scarsdale, New York, 21 June
1795	Graduated from Columbia College, New York
1803	Elected to New York State Assembly
1804	Elected to U.S. House of Representatives
1804	Appointed to New York State Supreme Court
1807	Elected governor of New York
1816	Elected vice president
1825	Died, Tompkinsville, Staten Island, New York, 11 June

BIOGRAPHY

One of 11 children of a farm family, Daniel Tompkins graduated first in his class at Columbia College and became a lawyer. In 1797, he married Hanna Minthorne, whose father was a leader of the Tammany Society, the New York Republican political organization. Winning his first election in 1803, the handsome and popular Tompkins rose quickly in politics.

Republicans ran Tompkins for governor in 1807 as "the Farmer's Boy." During the War of 1812, opponents of the war controlled the New York state legislature. Governor Tompkins used his own money and made personal bank loans to fund the state's militia. His actions won public acclaim, but poor record-keeping created suspicions about his mingling of personal and public finances.

In 1816, New York Republicans supported Tompkins for president. When the Republican Caucus nominated James Monroe, the third in a string of Virginia-born nominees, it balanced the ticket with Tompkins. The 42-year-old Tompkins also seemed likely to breathe new life into the vice presidency. Monroe and Tompkins crushed what was left of the Federalist Party and ushered in a one-party "Era of Good Feeling."

Despite his relative youth, Tompkins suffered severe ailments resulting from a fall from a horse. Confined to bed, he considered resigning. At the same time, his finances deteriorated. New York failed to compensate him for his wartime expenses. Depressed, he started drinking heavily.

Poor health and shaky finances kept Tompkins away from Washington for most of his vice presidency. His prolonged absences seemed a dereliction of duty. When he did appear, he proved an inept and sometimes intoxicated presiding officer. Yet in 1820, he ran again for vice president and the ticket swept to victory unopposed.

In 1822, Congress passed a law allowing the government to withhold the salaries of officials who owed money to the government. One of these debtors was Vice President Tompkins, who thereby lost the salary he so desperately needed. His creditors then sued him. When jurors heard of his wartime sacrifices, they decided in Tompkins's favor. Tompkins then regained some of his former vigor and paid greater attention to his duties as vice president. Congress belatedly voted to settle his claims and restored his salary. Weary and ill but "relieved of his embarrassments," Tompkins retired from politics after his second term. He died just three months later.

THE CABINET

SECRETARY OF STATE
John Quincy Adams, 1817, 1821

SECRETARY OF WAR
John C. Calhoun, 1817, 1821

SECRETARY OF THE TREASURY
William H. Crawford, 1817, 1821

POSTMASTER GENERAL
Return J. Meigs, Jr., 1817, 1821
John McLean, 1823

ATTORNEY GENERAL
Richard Rush, 1817
William Wirt, 1817, 1821

SECRETARY OF THE NAVY
Benjamin W. Crowninshield, 1817
Smith Thompson, 1818, 1821
Samuel L. Southard, 1823

(Courtesy Library of Congress.)

William H. Crawford (1772–1834). Crawford was appointed secretary of war by President James Madison in 1815. He resigned to become secretary of the treasury. He retained this post in the administration of James Monroe.

As secretary of the treasury, Crawford effectively lessened the financial hardships brought on by land speculation which caused the panic of 1819. He initiated the Crawford Plan which offered an alternative to foreclosure of public land purchased by private citizens. Under the plan, debtors could either pay the debt within an eight-year period or gain title to the land that they had already paid for and forfeit the remaining land.

In the fall of 1823, Crawford suffered a stroke, which left him partially paralyzed and almost blind. John Quincy Adams invited Crawford to continue as secretary of the treasury, but he refused and retired to his home in Georgia. He served as a judge in the superior court of the northern circuit of Georgia until his death on 15 September 1834.

FAMILY

CHRONOLOGICAL EVENTS

30 June 1768	Elizabeth Kortright born	1803	Daughter, Maria Hester, born
16 February 1786	Elizabeth Kortright married James Monroe	23 September 1830	Elizabeth Monroe died
		4 July 1831	James Monroe died
5 December 1787	Daughter, Eliza, born		

◄ Elizabeth Kortright Monroe helped to get the Marquis de Lafayette released from prison, when her husband was the U.S. minister in Paris. She had an illness that did not allow her to pursue all the activities of a First Lady.

(Courtesy James Monroe Museum and Memorial Library, Fredericksburg, Virginia.)

The Monroes' daughter, Eliza (pictured right) often filled in for her mother. She had been educated at an exclusive French school, and she was much more formal than her popular predecessor, Dolley Madison. She and her mother did not make calls on the other ladies in Washington society nor did they welcome them at the White House. They became even more unpopular when they chose to have a private wedding for the younger Monroe daughter, Maria. After the death of her father and her husband, Judge George Hay, Eliza returned to Paris. She converted to Catholicism and probably spent her last days in a convent.

Maria was the first president's child to be married in the White House. She married Samuel Gouverneur, and they moved to New York. President John Quincy Adams later appointed her husband postmaster of New York. After his wife died in 1830, Monroe moved in with them. He died in their home on 4 July 1831. ▶

(Courtesy Library of Congress.)

ASH LAWN–HIGHLAND

James Monroe Parkway • Charlottesville, Virginia 22902 • Tel: (804) 293-9539

Located five miles south of I-64 and U.S. 250, just outside Charlottesville. Open daily March through October from 9 A.M. to 6 P.M., and November through February from 10 A.M. to 5 P.M. Closed Thanksgiving, Christmas, and New Year's Day. Admission fee, with discounts available for groups, students, and local residents. Special educational and art programs are available. For more information, write: Ash Lawn–Highland, Route 6, Box 37, Charlottesville, VA 22902-8722. A financially self-supporting historic house museum owned by the College of William and Mary, Williamsburg, Virginia.

Thomas Jefferson personally selected the site for Ash Lawn–Highland and sent his gardeners to start the orchards. It is only two-and-a-half miles from Jefferson's Monticello. (Courtesy Ash Lawn–Highland.)

In 1793, President Monroe and his family purchased Highland, a 1,000-acre estate located in the Blue Ridge Mountains of Albermarle County, Virginia. This plantation became Monroe's primary residence for the next 27 years. After his death in 1831, the estate's name was changed to Ash Lawn. Both names are now used in combination. The property remained a working farm until philanthropists Jay and Helen Johns opened it to the public in 1931. Jay Johns left the estate to the College of William and Mary, Monroe's alma mater, upon his death in 1974.

Since 1975, the college has initiated research, restoration, and preservation projects. In 1992, parts of the building were restored to their original appearance. Monroe's imported French furnishings, china and silver, and original portraits of family members and friends, are on display. Many of these furnishings were used by the Monroes during their White House residency. The grounds reflect early nineteenth-century American society and plantation life. Peacocks, sheep, and horses roam the property.

▲ *Spinning, weaving, tinsmithing, open-hearth cooking, candlemaking, and soapmaking are among the crafts that visitors can see from April through October in the kitchen, slave quarters, and outer buildings at Ash Lawn–Highland.* (Courtesy Ash Lawn-Highland.)

◄ *James Monroe died on 4 July 1831 at the home of his daughter and son-in-law, Maria and Samuel Gouverneur, in New York. His body remained in the Gouverneur family vault at Marble Cemetery in New York until 1858, when it was removed to Hollywood Cemetery in Richmond, Virginia.* (Courtesy Library of Congress.)

SUGGESTED READING

GEORGE WASHINGTON

The World of Young George Washington by Suzanne Hilton (Walker, 1987) is a delightful look at the early life and times of George Washington. (For junior high school.)

Milton Meltzer's *George Washington and the Birth of Our Nation* (Watts, 1986) is a well-balanced, clear narrative that places Washington and his career in the context of a developing nation. *George Washington* by Roger Bruns (Chelsea House, 1987) is an enjoyable, well-illustrated biography that emphasizes Washington's development as a leader. Thomas Fleming wrote *First in the Hearts* (Walker, 1984), a well-documented narrative of Washington's life from about age eleven. *The Washington Way* by Jeffrey Morris (Lerner, 1994) discusses key decisions by Washington and their effect on the development of the country. (For junior and senior high school.)

James T. Flexner's *Washington: The Indispensable Man* (Little, Brown, 1974) is an excellent one-volume version of his extensive four-volume biography. *The Invention of George Washington* by Paul K. Longmore (University of California Press, 1988) shows how the world shaped Washington as well as how Washington shaped the world around him. For a well-written political biography of the first president that also provides insight into life in the 1790s, see Richard N. Smith's *Patriarch* (Houghton Mifflin, 1993). *The First of Men* by John E. Ferling (University of Tennessee, 1988) is an outstanding biography that looks at Washington's personality and character to explain his success. *Martha Washington, Our First Lady* by Alice C. Desmond (Dodd, Mead, 1963) is a good biography of the First Lady. Miriam Bourne's *First Family* (Norton, 1982) is based on letters to and from George Washington and other family members and provides a look at family life in the eighteenth century. (For high school and adult.)

Two excellent videos on George Washington are *Meet George Washington* (Time-Life) and *George Washington, Founding Father* (A&E Home Video). (For all ages.)

JOHN ADAMS

Rebecca Stefoff's *John Adams* (Garrett Educational Corp., 1988) is a good introductory biography. *John Adams and the American Revolution* by Catherine D. Bowen (Little, Brown, 1950) is an excellent biography that covers Adams's early life up to the signing of the Declaration of Independence in 1776. (For junior high school.)

Page Smith wrote an excellent two-volume biography, *John Adams* (Doubleday, 1962), that provides insight into his family life as well as his political life. See *The Presidency of John Adams* by Ralph A. Brown (University Press of Kansas, 1975) for an excellent analysis of the Adams presidency. *The Adams Chronicles* by Jack Shepherd (Little, Brown, 1975) traces the history of four generations of the Adams family and is based on the PBS series of the same name. (For high school and adult.)

Mildred Criss's *Abigail Adams: Leading Lady* (Dodd, Mead, 1952) is a good introductory biography of a remarkable lady who was the only woman to be the wife of one president and the mother of another. (For junior high school.)

Abigail Adams by Phyllis L. Levin (St. Martins, 1987), based on Abigail Adams's correspondence, is an excellent biography that shows the American Revolution from a woman's perspective. (For high school and adult.)

THOMAS JEFFERSON

Suzanne Hilton's *The World of Young Tom Jefferson* (Walker, 1986) follows the development of Jefferson's philosophy and provides insight into the social mores and customs of the eighteenth century. *Thomas Jefferson* by Charles Patterson (Watts, 1987) is a short, well-researched, and well-written biography. (For junior high school.)

Roger Bruns's *Thomas Jefferson* (Chelsea House, 1986) presents a balanced view of Jefferson's life and politics. *The Jefferson Way* by Jeffrey B. Morris (Lerner, 1994) provides a thoughtful analysis of important decisions made during Jefferson's presidency and of their ramifications. Milton Meltzer's *Thomas Jefferson: The Revolutionary Aristocrat* (Watts, 1991) deals with many thorny political and personal issues, including Jefferson's relationship with his slave Sally Hemmings, with sensitivity and balance. Natalie S. Bober's *Thomas Jefferson: Man on a Mountain* (Atheneum, 1988) is a highly readable biography that presents Jefferson as an extremely talented and intelligent man. (For junior and senior high school.)

For an excellent yet readable biography of the man as well as the politician, see Alf J. Mapp's *Thomas Jefferson: A Strange Case of Mistaken Identity* (Madison Books, 1987) and *Thomas Jefferson: Passionate Pilgrim* (Madison Books, 1991), a two-volume set. Robert W. Tucker's *Empire of Liberty* (Oxford University Press, 1990) provides insight into the development of his political policies. *Jefferson and Monticello* by Jack McLaughlin (Holt, 1988) is a personal portrait focusing on Monticello and domestic life during the

Colonial and Federal periods. *Monticello, A Family Story* by Elizabeth C. Langhorne (Algonquin Books, 1987) is an enjoyable portrait of Jefferson and his family. (For high school and adult.)

An excellent video is *Thomas Jefferson, Philosopher of Freedom* (A&E Home Entertainment). (For all ages.)

JAMES MADISON

Susan Banfield's *James Madison* (Watts, 1986) provides a balanced view of Madison's youth and shows his development as a statesman. Jean Fritz's *The Great Little Madison* (G. P. Putnam's Sons, 1989) is a well-balanced introductory biography. (For junior high school.)

James Madison by J. Perry Leavell (Chelsea House, 1988) is an objective, well-written biography that emphasizes his constitutional leadership. *James Madison* by Alfred Steinberg (G. P. Putnam's Sons, 1965) provides personal as well as political insights into Madison's career. Robert A. Rutland's *James Madison and the Search for Nationhood* (Library of Congress, 1981) describes his efforts to establish the concepts of individual liberty and national union in the American Republic. (For junior and senior high school.)

Also by Robert A. Rutland is *James Madison* (Macmillan, 1987), an excellent, easy-to-read biography. *The Last of the Fathers* by Drew R. McCoy (Cambridge University Press, 1989) is a good general biography of the last of the Founding Fathers. Irving Brant's *The Fourth President, A Life of James Madison* (Bobbs-Merrill, 1970), an excellent consolidation of the author's six-volume biography, emphasizes Madison's years as president and elder statesman. (For high school and adult.)

JAMES MONROE

Rebecca Stefoff's *James Monroe* (Garrett Educational Corp., 1988) is a well-balanced introductory biography. *James Monroe* by Edwin P. Hoyt (Reilly and Lee Co., 1968) provides a straightforward look at Monroe's presidency, known as the Era of Good Feeling. (For junior high school.)

Harry Ammon's *James Monroe, The Quest for National Identity* (University Press of Virginia, 1990) is a thorough study of all aspects of Monroe's life. *The Presidency of James Monroe* by Noble E. Cunningham (University Press of Kansas, 1996) offers a detailed analysis of his presidential years. (For high school and adult.)

at a glance . . .

l

m

p

q

r

s

t

v

W

X